The Most Improbable International Cricket Team Ever

A True Story

Mary W. Schaller

ISBN: 978-1-09836-804-3

This book is dedicated to the memory of

Bill Drake

President, Deddington Cricket Club

Deddington, Oxfordshire, England.

He made the dream come true.

THE SOS CRICKET TEAM

1988

Back Row, L to R: Coach Johnathon Bigelow, Zen Mason, Kurt Bosc [with cap], Jamie Fox, Steven Fender, Keene Parker and Paul Miller.

Middle Row, L to R: Kaija Barlow, Carol Blosser, Katie Shirley, Kathy Robinson, Angela Kluwin, Kym Samuels, Molly Pfaff and Manager Mary Schaller.

Kneeling, L to R: Susan Linsert, Terri Anderson, Beckey Kelsey and Meaghan Parker.

Absent: Ellen Caskie, Elizabeth Dettmar, Libby Goodwin, Amy Pearson, Nick Rose, Sabrina Sandusky and Julie Zielaskiewicz. (Martin Schaller)

"What other sport is there which involves people dressing all in white and then throwing themselves around a muddy field?"

--Julian Knight, M.P.

Author of *Cricket For Dummies.*

Contents

PREFACE
A *Midsummer Night's Dream*

The Sports Editor of the WASHINGTON POST newspaper snickered. The secretaries at the British Embassy smiled and shook their heads. The Provost of Eton College in Windsor, England chortled at the very idea. The talk show host of the BBC Oxford Radio station was intrigued. Their own tour bus driver laughed out loud. Even their name – The SOS Cricket Team – sounded like a joke, while some of the parents expected that this whole cricket idea would peter out before April.

But the twenty-four teenagers from Fairfax County, Virginia were serious. Beginning in the cold, dark days of February 1988, this ragtag co-ed cricket team had no ball, no bat, no wicket stumps, no protective padding, no rule book, no uniforms, no practice field, no coach, no opposing team, and absolutely no idea how to play the game. The only thing they did have was an idea, and the determination to escape their two-week guided bus tour through England and Scotland for an unscripted afternoon to meet with British teens.

Five months later, the SOS Cricket Team pulled on their matching shirts, stood on the pitch of the Deddington Cricket Club in Oxfordshire, England and tossed a coin to play the game of their dreams. This is the story of their crazy journey into cricket history.

And every word of it is true.

CHAPTER ONE

January 1988

"Golden Lads and Lasses"

--Cymbeline

The letters SOS did not indicate a distress call for help, though it sometimes seemed that way. Rather, the initials stood for Shakespeareans Over Seas, which aptly described the group. The boys and girls, ranging in age from thirteen to eighteen, were members of a large Shakespearean drama class that met on Saturday mornings in the autumn and spring, and a two-week day camp during the summer. In their classes, they learned about the life and times of William Shakespeare by performing scenes from his many plays, using the original language. This unique program was sponsored by the Fairfax County (Virginia) Department of Parks and Recreation.

Fairfax is the largest county in the Commonwealth of Virginia, with a population slightly more numerous than the entire state of Rhode Island. Founded in 1742, it is one of the oldest counties in the United States. The citizens are considered to be "upwardly mobile" and the majority of the adult residents have college educations. The U. S. News & World Report's school rankings for 2016 rated the Fairfax County Public School system as fifth-best in the nation. Considering the high expectations of the families living in Fairfax County, the Parks & Recreation Department was always on the lookout for inventive new classes to offer the children. In 1980, when the idea of starting a Shakespeare class for secondary school age kids was first suggested, Tina Stephens, Director of the Youth Classes, raised her eyebrows.

"Shakespeare for fun? Do you think anyone will sign up for it?"

The class, titled "Shake Hands With Shakespeare," proved to be a surprise hit, with many of the students returning each semester. In 1985, one of the parents arranged for twenty of the advanced students to take a two-week bus tour of the Shakespearean sites in England and Scotland. This tour was a huge success, so three years later, a new group of parents led by Dr. Everett Goodwin, father of one of the girls, decided to send a second group over to the United Kingdom. The first group had called themselves the Innocents Abroad, which they were in every sense of the words. In the fall of 1987, the second group, younger and much more adventurous, chose the name Shakespeareans Over Seas "after about fifty name changes and a lot of shouting," recalled Kym Samuels, who had been a member of the classes for six years. Later, the cricket team abbreviated their name to the SOS.

As part of the pre-trip preparations, the group attended Cultural Sunday meetings at someone's home once a month in order to plan their trip, and to learn about the differences between the British and Virginians. It was at the January 1988 meeting that the teens' big dream first came up.

"Okay, people, you've got the tour schedule in your hot little hands. Now, let's talk about what else you may want to see or do while you are in Britain. Any suggestions?"

As if on cue, everyone turned and looked at fifteen-year-old Kathy Robinson, a high school sophomore, who was both highly intelligent and popular within the group. It was obvious that the teens had already discussed something of importance and had elected her to speak for them.

Kathy flashed one of her disarming grins. "Well, we were thinking that we'd like to meet some of the kids over there. You know, English teenagers. I mean, all these places on our tour look really interesting to visit."

She waved her copy of the proposed trip itinerary. "But we also want to get to know what the kids are like over there. Can we visit with some of them?"

Everyone else nodded.

"Is that going to be possible, do you think?" Kathy cocked her head and smiled even wider.

Her request was a deceptively simple one. Fulfilling it should have been easy except for the fact that the tour was ten days of jam-packed activities that would keep the kids going from eight o'clock in the morning to ten at night. That was exactly what their parents wanted. Keep the teens fully occupied every minute of every day so that they couldn't "get into any trouble." In between seeing the crown jewels at the Tower of London, visiting three castles in England and two more in Scotland, as well as several cathedrals, attending two plays, having a formal afternoon tea experience in one of London's snazziest hotels, seeing Shakespeare's birth place in Stratford-on-Avon, punting flat boats on the Cherwell River, visiting medieval colleges in Oxford, and swinging by Loch Ness in the Highlands of Scotland in search of the elusive monster, there was barely any time to breathe. The parents wanted their little darlings to collapse into bed every night as soon as they checked into their hotels. Some of the fathers even wanted to ditch the half-day free time in London in order to keep their children "safe." How and where could the Americans meet the local kids and be able to spend some time getting to know them? Certainly not in an English pub.

One of the things that united this particular group, besides their sincere love of acting Shakespeare, was sports. Fairfax County is a competitive, sports-mad community. These kids not only got good grades in school, but they were also programmed into a lot of after-school activities – usually having something to do with a ball. Among the six boys and eighteen girls were a wide variety of athletes: soccer players, hockey queens, neighborhood pool team swimmers, basketball players, and one boy played on the varsity football team of the elite Thomas Jefferson High

School for Science and Technology. There were also a varsity tennis player from a private girls' school, baseball players, a gymnast, softball players, track and field athletes, lacrosse players, and two girls who were serious ballerinas. All of them – even the four non-jocks – knew the value of practice and hard work.

Their daunting tour schedule was not yet set in stone. There was some wiggle room, if we could find something educational that the teens could do which would enable them to meet and mingle with English kids. The words "something educational" were paramount. That would please the parents. Whatever they did had to be constructive and done in a controlled environment. No wandering off into the woods or pubs.

Then, from a distant time, a memory arose. In July of 1985, during the Innocents Abroad trip, one of the boys had purchased a child-sized cricket set as well as a regulation-size cricket ball at a Woolworth's store in Stratford. That evening, while staying at a youth hostel in London, twelve of the Innocents attempted to play a game of cricket, coached by their bus driver. They had a wonderful time, trying to hold the bat down instead of up and the pitchers trying to keep their arms straight while throwing the rock-like ball. Midway through their improvised game, one of the boys slugged the ball extra hard, and the child's bat split into three pieces. The kids were upset and vowed to buy another bat at the first opportunity. Sadly, that opportunity never happened during the rest of their tour, but the memories of that half-game lingered on.

Three years later, a friendly game of cricket might be just the way for the Shakespeareans Over Seas to actually meet some of the local kids.

"Okay. What would you say if we could arrange for you to play a game with some English kids?"

The group perked up.

"What sort of game?" Kurt Bose asked. At fifteen, Kurt dreamed of becoming an engineer. His mind was extremely analytical – that is, when he wasn't falling in love, which happened to him with surprising frequency.

"Well, since we are going in July, the national summer game in England is . . . cricket."

The room went completely silent. Not a tour schedule sheet rustled. Then Ellen Caskie, who was just two months' shy of thirteen and in the seventh grade, raised her hand.

"So, what's cricket?"

The game of cricket is uniquely British, although nowadays, the best players come from India, Pakistan and the Caribbean islands. No one is exactly sure when the game was first invented, but cricket has been played in the southern part of England for over five hundred years. Legend has it that the game was concocted during the Middle Ages by a group of bored shepherd boys, who were supposed to be watching their flocks of sheep. Sheep, being nature's best lawn mowers, tended to do nothing much except eat grass, which gave the shepherd boys a lot of time to do something else. The very name of the game – cricket – comes from an Old English word "cricc," meaning "staff" or "crook," an implement that shepherds used a lot while tending their sheep.

At its very basic level, cricket is a stick-and-ball game, however over the course of five centuries, it evolved, and became more precise and refined. One of the earliest written mentions of cricket is found in a 1597 court case in Guildford over a disputed ownership of a plot of land where, the plaintiff declared, "diverse of his fellows did runne and play at creckette." In 1611, a Puritan magistrate in Siddlesham, Sussex fined two parishioners 12 pence each [a hefty sum in the 1600s] for deliberately missing Easter Morning services in order to play cricket. In fact, court records show that the Puritan ministers often had great difficulties in keeping their flocks from playing cricket on Sundays, since Sunday was the only day in the week that most people had any leisure time. Though the specific game of cricket is not found in any of William Shakespeare's plays, it is not beyond the realm of possibility that the Bard knew how to play the game. He was fined for missing Sunday Divine Services on several occasions.

In the beginning, the shepherd's crook or stick was held down touching the ground, looking much like today's field hockey stick, and the bowler, i. e. pitcher, rolled or "bowled" the ball underhanded across the field towards the batter. Over the centuries, the stick changed shape from a rounded crook to a paddle-shape, but it was still held in a downward position. From the earliest days, it was the bowler's intent to knock over the wicket, a sheep's pen gate, which the batter tried to defend. When a form of the shepherds' game worked its way into the streets of the towns, the wicket gate was replaced by a three-legged stool which the bowler attempted to knock over and the batter tried defending it with his stick.

Cricket continued to evolve slowly during the seventeenth century, despite the Puritans' efforts to eradicate the game during the years of the Commonwealth [1649 – 1660]. Once the Stuart kings returned to the Throne in the jolly person of Charles II, the game of cricket quickly grew in popularity. King Charles not only loved wine, women and song, but he was also passionate about gambling. In 1660, interest in cricket moved up several notches when the gamblers of the Court and countryside began to bet on anything and everything about the game from the scores of runs, to the number of wickets bowled over, and even how many fist fights would break out during a match.

In the eighteenth century, as the city of London expanded, the availability of large grassy fields grew smaller. Because cricket requires a field of turf, the gentlemen of the Court realized that they needed to create suitable playing grounds within the increasingly crowded city. So, they formed several cricket clubs that maintained privately-owned plots in the fashion best suited for the game. The most famous cricket club of all was founded by several members of the nobility in 1774. Their playing field, owned by a successful wine merchant and professional bowler named Thomas Lord, was located near Marylebone Street, so the club members called themselves the Marylebone Cricket Club, and the playing field became known as Lord's Cricket Field, or simply Lord's. Since then and up to the present, Marylebone Cricket Club, also known as the MCC, has been the official keeper of the rules or Laws of Cricket. And Lord's Cricket Ground became as important to the world of cricket as the Wimbledon Lawn Tennis Club is to the game of tennis.

More relaxed cricket matches were played out in the country on village greens, usually within a short walk to a public house where after-game refreshments were served. The MCC had recognized county cricket by 1839.

During the early centuries of the game, underhand bowling was the norm, but that changed in 1745 when the first recorded game played by women took place. According to an account reported in the Reading MERCURY newspaper, the young women of Branley played a game of cricket against the young women of Hambledon, and "the girls bowled, batted, ran at catches [sic] as well as most men in that game." The only recurring problem that the women encountered was their bowling technique. Their long skirts tended to impede a clean underhanded toss of the ball.

One of the players was Christina Willes. When it was her turn to bowl, she decided to throw the ball overhand instead, and she discovered that the ball then behaved in a more satisfactory manner. Christina's brother, John Willes, was an expert cricketer who played for several clubs, and he saw that the ball both bounced and spun much better using his sister's technique. John made cricket history when he introduced overhand bowling at the next county game. Of course, there was an uproar among the cricket purists, mainly referees, but many other bowlers tried throwing the ball overhand, and quickly discovered that they preferred it.

Finally, in 1864, the overhand bowling method was legalized in the Marylebone Cricket Club's Book of Cricket Laws. During the long reign of Queen Victoria in the nineteenth century, the game of cricket followed the British Army around the growing British Empire, and it spread out across the globe. At home in England, the popularity of the game expanded as boys and girls learned to play at their schools, although cricket has always been more popular with schoolboys than with the girls.

In 1988, cricket seemed to be the logical way for the sports loving SOS to meet the British. Now all the Yanks had to do was learn how to play the game.

Kaija Barlow is ready to bat at Rutherford Field, Fairfax County, Virginia.
(Paul Miller)

CHAPTER TWO

February 1988

"Speak The Speech, I Pray You, As I Pronounce It To You."

Hamlet

The vast Fairfax Public Library system did not carry any books specifically about the game of cricket – at least not in 1988. Nor was there anything like Google, Amazon or the user-friendly Internet available at that time, where information about the game could have been accessed. The only thing near at hand was a small book titled, "The Story of CRICKET," which was published in England by the Ladybird Books series for young children. This thin volume had once belonged to my now-adult son when our family had lived in London for four years. Besides giving a brief outline of the history of the game, the book had a drawing of the fielding positions. One look at this illustration was going to send the fledgling SOS team into hysterical laughter.

Telling an Englishman that "Cricket is like baseball" is enough to cause the average Brit to gag into his teacup. Nevertheless, it was the best and fastest way for these Little League-trained kids to learn the basics of the game. But first, they had to learn the language.

Cricket has an entire dictionary of arcane terms that have absolutely no meaning to the average American. That includes the names of the myriad fielding positions. The SOS February Cultural Sunday meeting was ear-splitting, especially since the host mother had provided the teenagers with plates of sugar-loaded Valentine cookies. At this point in time, the team still had no equipment, no practice field, no coach and no clear idea of what they were getting into.

I cleared my throat. "Okay, people, let's talk cricket."

Instant attention.

"Right now, we don't have any cricket gear, but Libby Goodwin's dad is going to England in a couple of weeks and he's agreed to pick up some bats, balls and wickets for us."

Hand in the air. "What's a wicket?" Keene Parker asked. He was tall for his fifteen years, and he had played baseball for most of his young life.

"It's a set of sticks in the ground behind the striker."

More hands in the air. "What's a striker?" It was going to be a long afternoon.

Deep sigh. "Okay, everybody, listen up. Cricket is something like baseball and soft ball, except it isn't."

"So what is it?" asked several people at once.

One thing about the SOS – they were a noisy bunch, and they seemed to spend a great deal of time trying to outshout each other. But what else could you expect when you put twenty-four experienced Shakespearean actors in the same room and feed them sugar cookies?

"Okay. In a nutshell – and you may want to take notes here – with baseball you have the pitcher. In cricket, you have the bowler."

"Like nine pins bowling?" Katie Shirley asked. She was also fifteen, a sophomore and precocious.

"No, it's like throwing the ball. Next, the batter is called a striker, for obvious reasons. The catcher is called the wicket keeper, because he or she acts like a catcher in baseball."

"So, what's a --?"

Moving along quickly. "Like I said, a wicket is a set of three sticks in the ground with two little sticks balanced on top that the batter has to keep the bowler from knocking over. Got that? That's why we have to get our stuff from England. They don't sell it here in the local sporting goods stores."

"Yeah," drawled eighteen-year-old Nick Rose, the team's only Senior student. "I can just see me walking into Herman's Sporting Goods and saying, 'Hi! I'd like to buy three cricket wickets, please.' "

The room erupted into howls of laughter.

"Actually, it sounds more like we're baking a cake," remarked Kym, who was gifted with a wicked sense of humor. "You know, like you can beat the batter in a bowl?"

More laughter. And I hadn't even begun naming the esoteric fielding positions.

"People, do you want to learn to play cricket, or not?"

"Sorry, Mrs. Schaller." Kathy soothed the mob, "Come on, guys. Let's get serious."

Sighing. "I know that the game's terms sound funny, and there are lots more to come, but please understand something. The English may speak the same words that we do, but they don't always mean the same thing. For instance, if you went into a snack shop and asked for a bag of potato chips, you'd get French fries."

"What?" Elizabeth Dettmar wrinkled her nose. She was fifteen years old and one of the quietest persons in the group. "Why?"

"Because the word 'chip' means a fry."

"So how you would get a potato chip?" rumbled Jamie Fox from the back of the room. At fifteen going on sixteen and already close to six feet tall, this football star was perpetually hungry.

"You would ask for a bag of crisps. And if you are looking for cookies, they wouldn't know what you were talking about, either."

"Don't they eat cookies in England?" asked Amy Pearson, a fourteen-year-old freshman. She looked worried.

"Of course, they do. In fact, the English make some of the best kinds of cookies. But, in England, cookies are called . . . biscuits."

More cries of disbelief. These kids were Virginians, used to Southern cuisine delights like corn bread, hush puppies, and buttermilk biscuits, dripping with honey.

"So, what do they call our biscuits over there?" Kurt wanted to know.

"The closest things are scones, which are delicious when served with strawberry jam . . . and clotted cream."

"Yuck!" Sabrina Sandusky wrinkled her nose. At fourteen, she was the princess of the group. "Who would want to eat something that had spoiled?"

"Clotted cream isn't what you think it is. It is like a very thick, stiff whipped cream, beaten with sugar."

Kathy's brown eyes grew large. "Sounds yummy."

"Okay, people, can we get back to cricket now? I have a diagram here of what the cricket field looks like and what the fielding positions are, because most of you will be playing those positions."

Kathy took the sheaf of handouts and passed them around. There was silence for about sixty seconds, until the names of the positions sank in through their overly-sugared brains.

A few of the girls began to feel nervous. This cricket game suddenly looked more real. Carol Blosser stared at the paper in her hand. "When we first started talking about forming a cricket team, I was pretty apprehensive," she recalled years later. "I was the most unathletic kid on the planet."

Hands in the air.

"A gully?" Kurt asked. "There's supposed to be a gully in the middle of the field? What do we do? Jump over it? Is that part of the game?"

"No, it's not a dip in the ground. It's the name of the important field position that is halfway between the two wickets."

"Cricket wickets," whispered someone with a snicker.

Skipping along faster. "And I have no idea why it's called the gully. You have to understand that this game has been played for five hundred years and a lot of words have changed over time. Like the word 'silly.' Look at your paper. See on the side of the bowler? It says 'silly mid off.' Silly used to mean the word 'skilly' a couple of hundred years ago in England. And that meant 'smart.' So, a silly mid player would be an intelligent fielder, who is standing in the mid-field position. And 'off' would mean on the offside of the batter, or something like that."

"So that means you need to have a smart ass in the shortstop position?" Suzen Mason, known as Zen, asked with a glint of mirth in her eye. At sixteen and one of the group's free spirits, she was a Junior and was already looking at college brochures.

More laughter.

"Watch your language, Zen. Let's keep it polite."

"Sorry, Mrs. Schaller." Though her grin indicated that she was far from sorrowful.

"Get your silly mid off my –" Julie Zielaskiewicz began. Sixteen years old and the eldest girl in the SOS, Julie constantly worked hard to try to sound 'with it.'

"That will do, Julie. Okay, let's move on, folks."

"Silly cricket wickets," somebody whispered. More giggles.

Hand in the air. Kathy tried to return order.

"Mrs. Schaller. Can you please explain what a 'square short leg' does?"

"It's a three-legged cricket wicket looking for a dance partner," Kym whispered to no one in particular.

More whoops of laughter.

Clearing throat. "Look, folks, I didn't make up this game, and you need to start taking it seriously if you intend to play it – five months from now."

Hand in the air.

"How about we take these papers home and we can read about it then?" Kathy suggested, glaring at several of her teammates. "So, have we got a coach yet?"

"Working on that."

Two of the chaperons for this trip were a young couple named Brenda and Johnathon Bigelow. Johnathon had been my production assistant a decade earlier when he was in Eighth Grade and I was directing "The Hobbit" for my children's elementary school's Spring play. Over the years we had stayed in touch. Among Johnathon's many accomplishments were the facts that he had played baseball throughout his teen years, and I knew I could depend on him. Now in his late twenties, he was just the kind of guy whom the kids would like: young enough to be fun, but old enough to command respect.

Now all I had to do was talk him into taking on the cricket coaching job.

Another hand in the air.

"Do you know who we're going to be playing?"

"Working on that, too." Actually, I didn't have a clue at that moment.

Hand in the air. Zen had a look of mischief in her eyes.

"Why don't we ask we ask Eton to play a game?"

Ye gods! Why don't we ride unicorns onto Eton's hallowed fields and play polo with the cricket bats?

"Who's Eton?" Amy wanted to know.

"Only the top boy's school in England," Nick answered, with a lift of his eyebrow.

Eton College, located near to the town of Windsor, was founded in 1440 by King Henry VI. Over the centuries, Eton was the alma mater of twenty English Prime Ministers, as well as numerous sons of royalty from around the world, including Prince Charles' sons, Prince William and Prince Harry. Several Nobel Prize winners got their academic starts at Eton, as well as great literary figures such as the poet Percy Shelley, who literally left his mark at Eton by blowing up a tree with gunpowder in the South Meadow. The legendary Duke of Wellington, who defeated Napoléon's bid to rule the world, had also graduated from Eton, and the grand old Duke occasionally returned to his old school to watch the boys play . . . cricket. It was while enjoying a cricket match on the "playing fields of Eton," that the Duke remarked to an associate, "There goes the stuff that won Waterloo." In later years, that chance remark was turned around a bit and became the famous quotation that "The Battle of Waterloo was won on the playing fields of Eton." With a yearly tuition of a whopping 42,501 English pounds [in 2020], Eton was strictly for the gifted, talented and the most elite boys in the world.

"I don't think that –"

"We could write a letter to Eton, saying that we challenge them to a game," Zen continued.

"They'd cream us in the first five minutes," Nick pointed out.

"No, they wouldn't," Zen protested with a huge smile. "They would be so dazzled by our beauty, they would be too stunned to concentrate on the game."

"They wouldn't be dazzled by my beauty," Kurt muttered to himself. No one looked at him. The sixteen girls in the room gave Zen their complete attention.

"We could wear short shorts," suggested fifteen-year-old Kaija Barlow, the group's blond bombshell-in-waiting.

"They're probably so horny, they'd lose it," added one of the others.

"Oh, please," Keene growled under his breath, plainly embarrassed.

Loud clearing of throat. "NO, you could not wear short shorts at any time. You'll be wearing long, white pants."

"Aww, nuts!"

"White pants?" Ellen asked, but no one seemed to hear her.

"But can we ask Eton to play us?" Zen persisted, unwilling to let go of this daring idea.

"Let's take a vote on it, okay? All in favor of asking Eton to play cricket with us, raise your hands."

Seventeen hands went up in the air. The eighteenth girl, Becky Kelsey, was at her boarding school in Connecticut. She had been a summer Shakespearean for the past three years. On the other hand, the six boys looked glum.

Deep sigh. "Okay, here's what you will do, Zen. YOU will write a polite letter to the headmaster of Eton College, explaining who we are, and you ask him, very respectfully, if we may play their least experienced team. That would probably be the younger boys in the middle school. Please bring me a draft of your letter to Shakespeare class next Saturday, so I can take a look at it. Then I'll give you the address. Are you willing to do that?"

"Sure!"

The girls in the room whispered excitedly among themselves. The six boys continued to look disgusted.

"This'll be a real sticky wicket," Nick said to no one in particular.

The pace picked up between February and the next SOS meeting in March. Libby's dad returned from London with the promised sporting equipment that included a ball – only one ball. If we ever lost it during practice, the team would be in serious trouble. They needed a second ball quickly. After a depressing round of phone calls to the local sporting goods shops, it appeared that there were no cricket balls to be had in the

Washington Metropolitan area, and the store clerks had no idea where I could order one. None of them sounded very interested in cricket at all.

However, on the plus side, Johnathon rose to the occasion and agreed to be the coach.

"Johnathon approached the cricket game as he would any other entity – he got a book . . . lots of them," said his wife, Brenda. "Keep in mind, there were not an abundance of books on the subject of cricket in Northern Virginia, but he managed to find all there were." Several days later, he phoned.

"Have we got any bats and stuff?"

"Yes! One regulation bat, one regulation wicket set and exactly one regulation cricket ball."

"We're going to need a couple more balls."

"I'm working on it." Scribbled a reminder on a sticky note and tacked it to the wall by the phone.

"And I need a rulebook. I get the batting and the running part, but I never heard of half these terms, like 'bowling a maiden over.' That can't be what it sounds like."

"I'm working on it." Scribbled a second note and added it to the first.

The nice thing about living in Northern Virginia is having Washington, DC just across the Potomac River. And the very nice thing about having the Nation's Capital nearby is that the city is home to one hundred and seventy-seven foreign embassies. One of the largest of these belongs to the British. The operator at their embassy switchboard was extremely helpful, and thankfully she didn't laugh out loud when I asked how our team could get an official cricket rulebook. She patched me through to a gentleman named Mr. Copes, who spoke with a very plummy British accent.

"So, you have some youngsters who are looking to play cricket?" he asked.

"Yes." I didn't mention that most of the team were girls and that they wanted to take on the boys from Eton. "We have some equipment, but we desperately need a rule book. Do you have any idea how we could get one?"

"Jolly good!" he responded. Clearly, Mr. Copes liked cricket. "Let me see what I can do for you. Please leave me your telephone number and I will get back to you. It may take several days."

"Wonderful!" That was easier than expected.

The next weekend, my husband, Marty, and I had dinner with old friends, John and Carol Bessette, at our favorite Chinese restaurant. Over platters of Sweet and Sour Pork and General Tso's Chicken, our friends listened sympathetically to my woes of managing a clueless co-ed cricket team.

"Well, what do you need?" Carol asked.

"Everything! A team to play, a place to play in England, the rule book, a practice field here and mostly, more cricket balls. We only have one."

The Bessettes looked at each other, and smiled. "We have a friend in Oxford who might be able to help you," Carol said. "He's the president of a cricket club over there. At the very least, he can get you a few more balls."

"Would his team like to play a short game of cricket in July with a co-ed team of teenagers from Fairfax ?"

"There is no such thing as a short game of cricket," John observed with a chuckle.

"We'll ask him about getting some balls," Carol added. John smirked at that.

Even though it felt like I was dropping down a slick rabbit hole, at least now, there was a ray of light at the end of the tunnel. With Johnathon on board as a coach, the British Embassy getting us a rule book and the Bessettes' friend sending some more balls, things were beginning to look up. Now all the SOS needed was a practice field to use for the next couple of months.

The Most Improbable International Cricket Team Ever: A True Story

Fairfax County is home to approximately 360 parklands within its wide borders. Included are not only well-groomed parks with golf courses, tennis courts, skateboard ramps and ball fields of every description, but also wilder swaths of land for hiking, camping, nature trails, and the natural habitats for a large variety of flora and fauna native to Virginia, like poison ivy, skunks and copperhead snakes. Overseeing this fiefdom in the county is the Head of the Fairfax Parks Department, and in the Spring of 1988, the head was a much-overworked gentleman named Dusty Rhodes. His mother most likely did not christen her son "Dusty," but that nickname had stuck into adulthood. It was Dusty's unenviable job to parcel out the recreation fields to the county's plethora of sports clubs. He was none-too-happy when he learned what we needed.

"You should have put in a reservation last August," he began.

"I didn't know I was going to be managing a cricket team last August."

"Cricket? That's a Brit game, right?"

"Right, and we're going to be playing a team in England in July."

He leaned forward in his chair. "You mean this coming July?"

"That's right."

He looked at his calendar. "That's four months from now? You're going to pull together a cricket team in four months?"

"Yes, we plan to."

"Humm." Dusty opened a large spiral notebook and started flipping through pages. "Do you know how many ball clubs play here in Fairfax?"

Swallowing. "I imagine quite a lot."

"Hundreds. In the spring and summer seasons, the soccer teams alone are on every field I've got. Girl's teams -- all divisions, boy's teams – the same. Then there's the select soccer teams with some really aggressive parents, as well as the travel soccer teams. There's Little League baseball, adult baseball clubs and more soft ball teams than I can remember. The adult teams play far into late evening. By and large, they're pretty reasonable just as long as they don't drink beer in the parks."

He shook his head. "But it's the parents of the little kids' Wiffle ball, T-ball and PeeWee ball teams who are the worst. They want the best fields that are near the parking lots and the restrooms. And nobody, but nobody wants to be near anywhere that has snakes, ticks or poison ivy—three things that I can guarantee are in every park in the county by June." Dusty kept flipping through his notebook. "How big a field do you need?"

Good question! No idea! I took out the diagram of the field positions, and pushed it across his desk. Dusty pulled his glasses off the top of his head and studied the picture.

"There is no way I can find a field big enough for that oval. We don't even have an oval field. But . . ."

Held my breath.

"Looks like most of your action takes place on that rectangle in the middle."

"That's the cricket pitch. That's what they call it."

He squinted at the diagram. "Says it's twenty-two yards by twelve feet."

Does it?

He muttered, "Bowler, batter, wicket keeper, leg slip, backward short leg, silly point, gully –"

Nervous smile. "Those are some of the traditional names for the fielding positions. Think pitcher, batter, catcher, first base, second base, shortstop, outfield."

"I'll be damned. And your team knows this stuff?"

"They're working on it now."

"And how old are this bunch?"

"The youngest ones will be thirteen before we leave for England and the eldest is eighteen."

He raised his eyebrows. "That's quite a spread. And all these kids are in your Shakespeare classes that you teach for the County Rec Department, right?"

"Every one of them."

"And they all know Shakespeare?"

"Right now, the beginning class and the advanced one are preparing two versions of HAMLET for performance in May."

He chuckled to himself. "Well, the game's afoot," he quoted. "That was one of my favorite lines that Sherlock Holmes used to say to poor Dr. Watson. I guess your group could say the same thing."

"They will when they think of it."

Dusty shut his notebook and stood up. "Okay, Mary, I'll see what I can find for your kids."

"We'll take anything you can give us, Dusty."

Ancient Chinese curse: Be careful what you wish for; you may get it.

Batter Amy Pearson avoids the ball as Wicket keeper Terri Anderson waits to catch it. Katie Shirley, at the Slip position, is ready to back up Terri before the ball goes into the poison ivy at Rutherford Park. (Paul Miller)

CHAPTER THREE

March 1988

"We have strict statutes and most biting laws."
Measure for Measure

L ate one March afternoon, the phone rang. I hoped it would be Dusty with a practice field. Instead, it was Johnathon, who was hyperventilating.

"We're dead," he began.

"Didn't the British Embassy have the rule book? Mr. Copes told me that they got it yesterday."

"Oh, yeah, they had it."

"That was fast work."

"Would you believe it came from London in a diplomatic pouch? Straight from the gods of cricket at the Marylebone Cricket Club. And it isn't a rule book. Cricket doesn't have rules. This game has Laws – with a capital 'L.'"

Pause for a moment to marvel at the fact that the hallowed Marylebone Cricket Club had sent over a set of their rules . . . er. . . Laws in a diplomatic pouch. A vision danced through my fevered imagination of a proper British courier, dressed impeccably in a dark suit, a perfectly knotted Windsor tie and wearing a bowler hat, getting off a British Airways plane with his briefcase handcuffed around his wrist and our cricket rule book stashed inside next to some very important, urgent government documents.

Then back to reality "So, what's the problem? Why are we dead?"

"Do you know how many Laws this game has got?" asked the usually unflappable Johnathon.

"From the sound of your voice, I gather it's quite a lot."

"Yeah, there's forty-two of them."

"Yes, that is a lot, but I'm sure we can figure them all out."

"Not so fast. Under each Law are subdivisions."

"How many?"

"Anywhere from two to five or six."

"Each Law has five or six subdivisions?"

"That's not the half of it," Johnathon continued. "Under most of the subdivisions, there are two or three more sub-subdivisions of Laws."

"You have got to be kidding!"

"Nope! And the worst one is the last law in the book – Law 42. Basically, it says all unfair play is illegal."

"That sounds simple enough."

"You'd think so. I'd think so. But this particular Law has eighteen sub rules with a lot more sub-sub divisions, making up a total of seventy-three rules and regulations for unfair play. And that is only one Law! There are forty-one others. There's got to be several hundred rules to this game altogether."

"You're right. We're dead." Silence while pondering if we've made a ghastly mistake.

"And some of these are really crazy Laws. There's one in here that says something to the effect that the ball is not dead if it hits the umpire. It seems you can keep on playing even if the ump lies flat out unconscious."

A sense of the un-real began to descend. "Well, that's one way to win the game."

"The kids will go nuts if we tell them they have to memorize hundreds of these rules."

"Then we won't tell them, Johnathon. You just figure out how we play the basic game and when a question comes up, then we can check the rule book."

"Laws. It's a Book of Laws."

"Whatever!"

The second phone call was from Dusty Rhodes.

"Do you know where Rutherford Park is located?" he asked. "Not exactly," praying that it wasn't going to be at the far side of the county next to the West Virginia State line.

"It's on Guinea Road, just off Braddock Road. You know where Braddock Road is?"

It was one of the main thoroughfares going East-West across the county, and ten minutes from where I lived. "I think I know which park you mean."

"Can you meet me there in the parking lot tomorrow afternoon, say around two-thirty?"

"Of course!"

We have a field! We have a field!

Well, not exactly.

Dusty was pacing back and forth the next afternoon at two-thirty on the dot, looking like he would rather be at the dentist.

"This way." He started walking toward the grass without any opening preamble. Ahead of us were several beautiful playing fields, laid out one behind the other, stretching off towards the far end of Rutherford Park. Any one of these would be perfect for us.

Dusty halted before we got to the backstop of the first field. He made a ninety-degree turn to the right and headed off toward the waste ground that lay between the perfect fields and Guinea Road.

"Here." He stopped in the center of a plot featuring tufts of rough grass, a lot of pebbles in the bare, damp patches, with woods on either side of a narrow field about the length and width of three tennis courts. "This is the best I can do for you."

"Here?"

One side was bounded by a creek, filled with gurgling water and large rocks. Opposite was woodland, no doubt full of snakes and thorns. Guinea Road, with whizzing afternoon traffic, cut off the top end of the ground, leaving the fourth side that faced the perfect playing fields.

Dusty nodded. "Sorry I can't give you one of those fields." He pointed over to the perfect ones. "They're booked up solid with a couple of softball teams and a baseball team. Those teams start coming in here just before four o'clock and they play until dark. But this here ground is all yours for as long as you want it, whenever you want it."

Keep smiling and nodding so I don't cry.

"And you won't have to pay for the use of it, since you already work for the County," Dusty continued. "And you're covered by insurance here."

Insurance? Hadn't even thought of that!

"I'll tell the landscaping boys to keep this area mowed for you. Now there's one more thing . . ."

What else could go wrong?

"That creek is the Long Branch. Ever heard of it?"

"No, is there something wrong with it?" Was the water toxic? Did it glow green at night?

"Right now, it looks pretty tame, but after a good rainstorm, it will be flowing pretty fast and much higher."

"How high?"

"Might flood your field a bit."

Which explained why the ground looked a little muddy. This was a flood plain.

Dusty hurried on. "But it drains off fast, and that's what you have to watch out for."

"Watch out for what?" Invading crocodiles?

"If your ball goes into the creek when it's running high, your ball will be washed downstream for about three miles before it empties into Lake Accotink. And I don't recommend that any of your kids jump into the creek and try to get it back when the Branch is high."

He was so full of good news.

"You better plan on having some extra balls."

"Working on it."

The Long Branch Creek at low ebb. It often flooded these banks after rain.

After Dusty beat a hasty and guilt-ridden retreat, I wandered around our new home turf. At least the ground was flat, although pebble strewn. The team could place their rectangle pitch a little more to the left of center, away from the raging Long Branch. Batting could be a problem, depending how well the kids learned to hit the ball. If the batters faced Guinea Road, there would be a chance of hitting a homeward-bound car. If the batters faced in the opposite direction, there was good chance that they could brain a baseball player in the nearby field.

While I was disappointed by our shoddy field, some of the SOS team members felt differently about it. Years after the fact, Carol Blosser wrote, "I have such vivid sensory memories of being in Rutherford Park in the springtime. The trees and plants blooming . . . everything was so green."

Now that we had a field of sorts, what the team needed was some markers to define the boundaries of the rectangle pitch. Dusty didn't offer the services of the grounds crew and their chalk marking cart. No point if the field flooded every so often. Looking around for inspiration, I spied large orange cones beside the parking lot.

Cones! Little ones could be put out and taken up after the team was finished practice for the day. Our local home office store carried cones. At least something was going to work out.

With the coming of the school Spring Break, the SOS Team were in high spirits for the March Cultural Sunday meeting. Thankfully, this host mother had taken my advice not to serve anything with sugar. Bowls of popcorn and salty pretzels circled around the room. This month, Becky joined the group, being home for Easter break from her boarding school.

"Okay, folks, let's get down to business. We have a lot to cover today."

"Did you bring the bat?" Kurt wanted to know. "Libby said her dad got the stuff."

The cricket gear lay hidden in a duffle bag under my chair. "All in good time. We need to talk about your team uniforms first."

General uproar. No one had mentioned wearing a uniform. When the hubbub died down, Becky, who wore a variety of uniforms daily at her school, raised her hand.

"What sort of uniform?"

"The traditional cricket uniform is white pants, white shirts, white vee-neck sweaters, white socks, white—"

"Ooooh! Not white!" Sabrina moaned. "We'd look awful!"

"Well, you have to wear something nice out on that field. After all, you will be representing the United States of America."

That pronouncement shocked them into silence for about thirty seconds.

"Oooh! Not red, white and blue!"

"So predictable!"

"We'd look like we were going to the beach!"

Mary W. Schaller

"We'd look silly."

The noise settled into a low hum.

"Well, what do you want to wear? You can't go out on that field in your undies!"

The girls giggled, while the boys looked a little embarrassed.

"Why not?" Zen had on her mischievous look again. She loved to stir the pot on occasion. "It would certainly be a distraction – especially if we get to play the boys from Eton."

Keene grumbled under his breath.

Clearing my throat. "Have you heard from Eton yet, Zen?"

"Not yet, but it's probably too soon. I just mailed the letter two weeks ago."

"We're going to play Eton?" Becky looked a little alarmed.

"Over my dead body," Steve Fender, age thirteen, mumbled to no one in particular.

"We've asked them," fifteen-year-old Angela Kluwin soothed Becky. "We'll see."

"Okay, folks, no red, white and blue. So, what do you want to wear? It has to look like we're a team, not a bunch of people who just crawled out of bed."

"Well, not yellow. That's a terrible color," Kym ventured. There was general agreement.

"Not green! I do not want to look like an elf - again," said Ellen, who had played more than her fair share of elves and fairies in the Shakespeare class.

"How about -- black?" Zen asked.

General hubbub again.

"Why black?"

Zen shrugged. "Well, if the other team is going to be dressed in white, they'll be traditional, like the Laws of Cricket. So-o-o, we'll be in black, because we're the out-Laws."

General agreement, for once. A spatter of applause.

Sigh.

"Okay, folks, let's compromise. You can wear black tee shirts, but I would like you all to wear white pants. Just to show that we do know what the cricket tradition is. We don't want to be rude."

Wearing tee shirts with special designs was the usual practice with the Shakespeare classes. Tee shirts inspired teamwork and made everyone in the cast feel that they were a part of something special, even if they had only one line to say in the play. The kids in the Shakespeare classes had been wearing and collecting play production tees for over five years. When the first Shakespearean tour group went to England in 1985, their shirts were royal blue with a white Tudor rose logo, and they also had small blue duffel bags with their names embroidered on them. The idea of a group tee shirt was not unusual. What was unusual was the color.

"Black shirts and white pants?" Zen repeated, looking around at the group. "I think we can do that."

Sigh. "All in favor of a black tee shirt and white pants as your team uniform raise your hands."

Twenty-four hands in the air. For once, they had all agreed on something without a noisy debate. Several of the more artistic girls volunteered to come up with an SOS logo for the next meeting.

Hand in the air. "Do we get duffle bags too?" Steve wanted to know. His older sister, Kim, had been a member of the Innocents Abroad trip in 1985, and Steve recalled her personal duffle.

"Of course!"

General cheering. More popcorn tossed at each other.

"Okay, next – the good news. First, we have a coach. It's your chaperone, Johnathon Bigelow, and you'll like him. Plus, he knows what he's doing. Second, we have a practice field. It's in Rutherford Park on Guinea Road. Third – write this down, please – cricket practice will start on the Tuesday after Easter at 4 PM. That's April 5th. Please try to be on time."

With the welcome announcements of a real coach, a real field and a start date for practices, the group realized that this cricket game idea was really going to happen.

"I was delighted when the cricket idea came up. It was quirky and unusual," recalled Terri Anderson, who was fifteen years old. "But I was also dubious that a bunch of Shakespearean drama kids could pull it off."

"And finally –" I reached down and pulled up my bag. "I have your cricket gear – here!"

General pandemonium.

Pulling out the wicket pieces. "Okay, okay, listen up, people! This is your wicket. Nick, stand up so I can demonstrate – and no cricket wicket jokes please."

Nick uncoiled his slim frame from the floor beside Becky. I handed him the three sticks and asked him to hold them up.

"These sticks are called stumps, probably because the first wickets were made out of tree stumps – or whatever. They are stuck in the ground at the backline of the cricket pitch. Like so . . ." Nick held up the three sticks. I produced two smaller sticks. "These little do-dads are called bails, and they perch on top of the stumps, like this."

A bit of wobbling and shifting of stumps, as well as dropping of bails followed, but Nick finally got the wicket together. He held it up carefully.

"The simple point of the game of cricket is to protect this wicket. The bowler – like a pitcher – throws the ball to try to knock the bails off the stumps. The batter or striker tries to protect the wicket by hitting the ball to kingdom come, or thereabouts, and then making runs back and forth until someone can get the ball back to the bowler. Everybody got that?"

Hands in the air.

"So, if that's all there is to cricket, why are there so many stupid terms that we have to learn?" asked Julie.

"It gets more complicated, trust me. You'll see, once we start practice. Okay, Nick, let's put the wicket away. Now, ladies and gents, here is the bat." I passed it around the room.

Whoops of glee. More reality. Several of the team members stood up and looked like they were ready to take a swing in the confines of the host's family room.

"Sit down, please, everyone. This thing is serious business."

"What kind of wood is this?" Jamie wanted to know, hefting the bat.

"Willow, I believe."

"Baseball bats are made of ash," said Kurt to no one in particular. "I wonder why cricket bats are made of willow."

"No idea, they just are. Take it on faith. Now, may I have the bat, please? We have to take good care of it. It's the only one we have."

Hand in the air.

"Are we going to use that bat at practice?" asked one of the younger members.

General hooting.

"No-o-o, we're going to practice with tennis rackets," giggled Zen.

"Okay, folks, that's enough. The answer is yes, we are going to be using this bat at practice for the next three months, and all of you will take tender, loving care of this bat. Everybody got that?"

General agreement.

With the bat and wicket stowed safely back in the bag, the time had arrived to introduce the most precious piece of cricket equipment that we had.

"Ladies and gentlemen, I present to you - our one, and only cricket ball."

A regulation cricket ball should be certified as a lethal weapon. It is slightly smaller than an American baseball in circumference, more compact and is therefore much harder. It is also nearly a half ounce heavier than a baseball. Unlike a baseball, a brand-new cricket ball is red in color and its leather skin is polished to a shine, making it spin faster through the air. A cricket ball, well-thrown by a champion bowler, can attain the speed of nearly ninety-four miles per hour by the time it reaches the batsman. And that is the other problem with a cricket ball. The distance between a baseball pitcher's mound and home plate is 60 feet and 6 inches. The approximate distance between the cricket bowler and the batsman is 58 feet. Therefore, a fast-moving cricket ball reaches the batsman quicker than a baseball reaches home plate, giving the cricket batsman less time to react. No major league baseball player has ever died after being struck by a baseball, however there are nine recorded cricketeers who have died on the field after being hit on the head by a cricket ball. Since there was no such thing as Google in 1988, no one had any idea of these grim statistics when team SOS met at Rutherford Park for their first practice.

Tuesday, April 5th was cloudy, chilly and hinting of a shower when the first team members showed up to learn all about cricket. The SOS was made up of students who attended two secondary schools, five different high schools and three middle schools. All of them were spread out the length and breadth of Fairfax Country, so very few kids showed up at the same time. Since the middle schools ended earlier, the younger members like Ellen Caskie, Carol Blosser, Amy Pearson, Sabrina Sandusky, Steve Fender and Susan Linsert stumbled out of cars and onto the field first. Despite the cold, grey afternoon, they were bright-eyed and raring to go.

They quickly helped to set up the orange cones as they measured out the twenty-two yard by twelve foot rectangle in the middle of the damp waste ground. Pounding the wicket stumps into place at the near end of the pitch was accompanied by loud chatter and giggles. They wanted to start batting right away.

By that time, a few of the older teens arrived, some chewing on power bars and other snacks.

"Let's play!" Jamie shouted.

"Where's the bat?" Kurt wanted to know.

The dreaded whistle blew across all the chatter. "Not yet! First, you have to warm up."

"I am warm," shouted Keene.

"No, you're not. You all have been sitting behind your desks since eight this morning –"

"Eight-thirty!" Kurt yelled.

Before anyone else could volunteer what time they had started school, the dreaded whistle blew again. "All of you need to warm up, to loosen up. I want you to run around that field. No crossing over in the middle. All the way around. Now go!"

Good natured grumbling. The team would argue over the size of a flea, if given the opportunity, but they saw the point of the run and it made them feel like they were really starting something BIG.

Johnathon had not yet arrived, so the team started around the field a second time. Johnathon's day job was the manager of a popular Mexican restaurant at Tyson's Corner, Fairfax's largest shopping mall. He promised to squeeze cricket practice in between the end of the lunch shift and before the dinner hours started. He and Brenda arrived just as the kids started on their third lap. Johnathon was greeted with cheers of relief.

Everyone was ready to start batting practice.

"Not yet," announced their new coach. "First, you have to learn how to catch this sucker." He held up the precious red ball.

"We know how to play catch," Terri informed him. Hers was the voice of practical reason in the group.

"No, you don't. Not this ball. This isn't a baseball or a softball. It's a cricket ball and it hurts if it hits you, so you'd better learn how to catch it without breaking any of your fingers."

That announcement got him instant attention – and blessed silence.

Johnathon continued. "The first thing you have to learn is that cricket players don't wear gloves. You have to catch this little ball barehanded."

"What?" several of the kids wailed.

"That's right," Johnathon continued. "If you are wearing any rings, take them off now."

"Does that include my nose ring?" Kym asked with a grin.

Johnathon didn't bat an eyelash. "Not unless you plan on catching this ball with your teeth – which I don't recommend. Okay, everybody, get into a circle. We are going to play catch."

For the next fifteen minutes, the team tossed around the cricket ball gingerly with a lot of "oops," "ows," "ouches," and assorted yelps.

"That hurts!'

"It stings."

"I think I banged my elbow."

"Can't we start with a tennis ball?"

"Nope." Johnathon was firm. "Here, catch!"

"Owie!"

Brenda made herself comfortable at a nearby picnic table and watched the practice. "When I first heard about playing cricket, I immediately romanticized the whole thing," she recalled. "But at that first practice I thought, 'Oh yeah . . . we are clueless, but what the hell?'"

Even Paul Miller caught the ball on occasion, and always with a big smile on his face. Cricket was the very first ball game he had ever played in his life. And the SOS was the only sports team he had ever been allowed to join.

Paul was older than everyone else on the team, because he had been one of those "special" kids who got caught in the cracks of public school administration. Paul had two strikes against him from birth. He had severe hearing loss and his eyesight was also extremely poor. Consequently, he spoke later than the average toddler and his speech was slurred. He spoke words the way he heard them. He understood what people said to him, but he had trouble responding in clear sentences. He had no idea what a clear sentence sounded like. And because of his deafness, his sense of balance was impaired. People thought he was slow and clumsy. None of these problems were recognized early on for what they were. Instead, Paul was classified as "mildly retarded," and put into encapsulated Special Education classes. He never sat in a "normal" classroom. His teachers told his parents that Paul could learn to be a janitor when he grew up.

But Mrs. Marlene Miller didn't buy that. As her son matured, she noticed that he was keen on the movies. He begged to see his favorites over and over when his parents got a home video machine. Paul exhibited an interest, not only in the story lines, but also in costume and set design. When his parents got him a simple camera, Paul found his niche. Despite his foggy eyesight, he was able to take very good photographs. His film and processing bills must have been astronomical, but photography was his salvation.

When Mrs. Miller saw the ad for the Shakespeare class in the Fairfax County Parks & Recreation booklet, she phoned Tina Stephens and told her about Paul. Tina called me and asked if I were willing to take on a "special" boy. I replied that I had no training in Special Ed, but I would treat him just like any other kid.

"Let's give it a try."

Though naturally shy, Paul bloomed in Shakespeare class. He got very small roles, which was just fine with him, and the other kids in the classes accepted him as "one of us." Now, four years later, Paul was going to travel with his classmates to England. His mom would be one of the chaperones. More importantly, from Paul's point of view, he was now a member of a real sports team – the SOS.

Paul never missed a practice during the next three months, and he got his turn at the bat, like everyone else. More importantly, Paul became the team photographer and his pictures caught the very essence of the SOS Cricket Team.

By the end of practice that first afternoon, everyone limped home with red, stinging hands, a few bruises from the ball and a new respect for the game of cricket. As Katie later observed, "Catching the ball is a lot harder than it looks compared to softball, and it comes at you faster."

Carol was an early victim. "My worst experience was being hit in the leg with the cricket ball."

Terri agreed. "Yowza! It did NOT feel like a baseball or softball."

Kym, never a sports jock, knew she had met her match. "I was very enthusiastic during the first practice, but then I realized that catching the ball hurt." Not wanting to give up on the game altogether, Kym opted to become one of the team's scorekeepers.

Practices were held twice a week, on Tuesdays and Fridays, unless it was pouring with rain. After a week devoted to nothing but gaining a new respect for their cricket ball, the team started batting practice, and that was when another snag arose.

When it came time to teach the team about batting, Johnathon, who had never hit a cricket ball in his life, just told the kids to "whack it as hard as a baseball while kind of holding the bat like a golf club."

"The bat swing was unusual and interesting to learn," Carol recalled. "I think it's a muscle memory I still have."

The Most Improbable International Cricket Team Ever: A True Story

Because of the traffic roaring up and down Guinea Road at the bottom of the cricket pitch, Johnathon had the bowlers start by keeping the baseball fields behind them. The batsmen faced the distant fields, and thus avoided batting a ball into a car. All went well until it was Keene's turn. Keene had years of practice slugging a ball with a bat. On this particular day, Jamie, the team's top bowler, hurled a fast one to Keene. Keene hit it with all his considerable strength. It flew high and long, over the heads of the girls who were fielding the mid-on and mid-off positions. It sailed over Steve, who was at cover point. And it landed within a hair of hitting a third baseman on the baseball field behind us. Ordinarily, Keene would have rejoiced at hitting a home run, but not this time.

A red-faced, puffing baseball coach came running up to us with our only ball in his hand.

"Just what the hell do you think you are doing?" he bellowed.

Team SOS froze. Johnathon was quick to reply.

"We're very sorry, sir. The kids here are just learning how to play cricket and we had no idea how long and how far the ball would go. Is your player okay?"

At the word, "cricket", the other coach stopped snorting. By this time, Keene joined them, still holding the bat. The baseball coach looked at our paddle bat, then at the team – all of whom looked scared – then at Johnathon and me.

"Cricket? Like the English game?"

"Yes, sir, exactly. We're getting ready to go to England and play a team there." As soon as we could find a team to play.

"Well, just don't bat in our direction. Cricket, eh?"

Bright smile. "Yes, why don't you stop by and watch us sometime?"

The coach nodded. "I might do that. I've always wondered what cricket was like. Well, good luck with that. Just hit your balls someplace else." Then he turned and went back to his baseball team.

Weakened knees. "Okay, Johnathon. Now what do we do?"

He stared at our pitch, then at our narrow field. "Okay, we'll move our pitch up closer to the ball fields, then we'll bat towards the road. It's the only thing we can do, unless you can get us another field."

"This is all we have."

"Okay, Keene, don't hit it as hard as you can. And we'll put more fielders down at the far end, nearer to the road."

And that's what we did. The SOS Cricket Team never again stopped another baseball team practice, nor did the batsmen ever hit the road, much less a moving vehicle. But our ball did do a lot of swimming in the Long Branch Creek.

Steven Fender shows good batting form, but his backswing hits the wicket, knocking over the bails. The umpire calls "hit wicket" and Steve is out.

(Johnathon Bigelow)

CHAPTER FOUR
Late April 1988

"Though she be but little, she is fierce."
A Midsummer Night's Dream

The SOS called her "The Mighty Mite," but that nickname didn't bother the little girl. At four feet, ten inches tall, Susan Linsert was not only the shortest member of the team, but she was also the youngest. She would not turn thirteen years old until mid-June, two weeks before the team took off for England. With her bouncing brown curls and dimples, Susan looked like everybody's sweet kid sister – until she put a cricket ball in her hands. Then this little powerhouse took off. Despite possible height problems, Susan was an enthusiastic basketball player and soccer lover. Now her athletic prowess transferred to cricket with ease.

By the time April appeared on the calendar, the team members had begun to sort out their favorite positions on the field. There were now four bowlers: Keene, Kurt, Jamie – and Susan. While the boys took long, loping runs up to the bowling crease [line] before throwing the ball, Susan opted for a short burst of speed followed by a throw that was low, fast, and true. Many of her pitches shattered the wickets behind the often-surprised batters. Very quickly, Susan won the respect of all her teammates, and she was proud to be called the Mighty Mite.

"The friends that I've made in the SOS are people I didn't even know existed. They are all interesting, funny and nice – and they have respect for other people," Susan wrote in a letter several later.

By now, most of the team were used to catching the ball, though some of the girls wore soccer gloves. "When we first started practice, they [the girls] were afraid. They'd get to the ball, and then scream and jump away from it," Johnathon observed. "Now they run and dive for it."

Susan Linsert, "The Mighty Mite", connects with the ball, but the huge pads will give her trouble when she runs. Behind her, Kaija Barlow, wicket keeper, waits for a miss. (Johnathon Bigelow)

With serious batting practice underway, the need for good fielders, especially wicket keepers, arose since the team had to avoid the baseball field behind them. Both Terri and Kaija discovered early on that they liked this position, and the girls would alternate with each other during the afternoon practices. "I was completely shocked that I wasn't half bad at being wicketkeeper," Terri recalled. Meanwhile, the rest of the team tried out such fielding positions as the "silly mid off" and "long leg". Molly Pfaff's favorite spot was the "Gully," just because she liked the name.

"Sometimes it was hard getting the rules across to the kids, especially when I had a hard time learning them myself," Johnathon acknowledged in an interview. His copy of the Marylebone Cricket Club's Book of Laws lived in his back pocket. "I've been teaching myself while I'm teaching them. We're literally learning the game as we go."

Johnathon's personal favorite rule in the book was Law 42, section 10 : "Any form of time wasting is unfair" and therefore illegal. The kids took this one seriously, so that all Johnathon had to do was yell, "Hey, you! Rule Forty-two!" and the errant team member would shape up.

"It's pretty much like 'Let's get out there and play,'" he added. "And when we're unsure, let's pull the rule book out."

Jamie concurred. "Cricket is a lot different than any of the games we have around here. There are a lot more rules to remember."

The four bowlers' biggest problem was remembering to keep their throwing arms straight. This was particularly difficult for all three of the boys, since they had been playing baseball for years.

"It is the oddest feeling to keep your elbows locked," Johnathon confessed. "After the first practice, my back was killing me, but we've all gotten used to it by now. The kids have shown a pretty strong interest in cricket from the start, and that's helped. It's a little surprising to me, but some of them like it better than the sports we play over here."

Fourteen-year-old Steve, the tall "long leg" fielder, agreed. "I like cricket. It's pretty much fun. I wanted to learn more about the English culture and what they do in their free time."

Jamie added. "I definitely like cricket better than baseball because I'm better at it than baseball. It's a little slow until someone gets a hit, then it picks up."

Everyone liked taking their turn at bat. The most difficult thing to learn was how to handle the bat. The team members were used to holding baseball bats over their shoulders. Cricket required the bat to be held "upside down," as one of the kids noted. The hand and elbow positions seemed a little uncomfortable at first.

As April progressed, a new problem reared its ugly, little green head – poison ivy. The team quickly discovered that their field was literally ringed by this nasty, itchy weed. Its presence created a greater incentive to catch the ball before it landed, especially in the wooded area to the left of the pitch. Meanwhile, on the righthand side, the Long Branch stream bubbled along. Fortunately, the water level remained low as the early Virginia summer days began to heat up. Whereas April seemed full of rain, May was mostly sunny and hot. Water breaks were more often, and longer. Happily, most of the pitch stayed dry and was shaded by tall trees.

"Is it this hot in England?" Amy asked on a day when the afternoon temperature headed towards ninety degrees. She lay flat on her back on the grass. Several other girls sat nearby, sipping water.

"Rarely. Summers in England are usually coolish and pleasant."

"Do they have poison ivy over there?" Ellen wanted to know.

"No, but they do have nettles in the underbrush."

"What do nettles do?"

"Mostly sting. But don't worry. You'll be playing on a real cricket field and they keep those fields nicely mowed and the underbrush far away." At least, I hoped so.

"Are there snakes? Or ticks?" Angela asked with apprehension.

"There are a few snakes, but they are mostly in the western part of the country and usually harmless. You won't see any on a cricket field. And England doesn't have ticks."

Zen joined the conversation. "You mean there'll be no tick-y wickets?"

Revived by a water break, batting practice resumed. The team had not yet tried to play an actual game, so Kym and Julie, the two scorekeepers, didn't have much to do, other than keep track of the numbers of hits that each of the batters made. It soon became obvious that Kathy was the best batter among the girls. Molly, Zen and Elizabeth were also good batsmen. Keene proved to be an "all-rounder," an excellent batsman as well as a top bowler. The SOS team was shaping up.

"Zen! Have you heard from Eton yet? Are we going to play the boys?"

"Haven't heard a word," she replied, slugging the ball into the Long Branch.

A dash to the creek's bank, a leap over the poison ivy and Kurt grabbed the ball that had lodged against a rock. The team now had two more balls, thanks to the Bessette's friend in England, but Johnathon wanted to keep the good ones until the team started playing a real game. Fortunately, the Long Branch remained very low.

"I've always wanted to go to England," mused Susan, after taking a long drink of water. "I've always been interested in the Middle Ages and Elizabethan times, so I want to see the castles." She paused, then added, "And the Loch Ness Monster."

Silent prayer that the Loch Ness Monster would be asleep on the day when the kids visited Scotland.

"I like the idea of meeting the people outside of a tourist setting," Kym added.

Zen grinned. "I like the idea of meeting the boys!"

"Hey, you girls!" Johnathon bellowed from the middle of the pitch. "Rule Forty-two!"

"Uh, oh! Here we go again!"

"My best memory of the SOS was the practices," Carol recalled. "There was a lot of laughter. I don't remember what was so funny, but it was."

Like the time Kurt showed up at a practice, cradling a ten-pound sack of flour. The flour bag was neatly wrapped in a blue baby blanket.

"Kurt! What have you got?"

Without hesitation, he replied, "It's my baby."

Some of the girls giggled. Kurt ignored them.

"Your baby? Please explain."

"It's for my Family Life class. For this weekend, we each have a bag of flour that we have to take care of. It's for a big-time grade," he added sheepishly.

Trying to keep a straight face. "You couldn't find a babysitter?"

"No, that's not allowed."

Some of the team members knew about the Family Life classes. Others were wide-eyed, and almost everyone caught a fit of the giggles.

"Okay, Kurt. Put the baby on the picnic table and let's start laps."

He signed. "I can't. She might roll off. And I can't run while holding her."

"You're talking about this sack of flour, right?"

"Exactly. It's my baby." He had been gently bouncing it up and down, as if to keep the flour quiet.

"Okay, Kurt. How about if I hold the flour—"

"The baby."

"I'll hold the baby while you run, okay?"

"Okay, but don't drop her or put her down." With the utmost care, Kurt handed over the blanket-wrapped bundle.

"I'm a mom, Kurt. I've done this before."

For the next hour, I patted the "baby", rocked the "baby" and even burped the "baby", while Kurt happily played cricket. No one dared to make any jokes about Kurt's baby.

At the end of practice, Kurt carefully reclaimed his baby and went home with it. One thing was very clear to every other member of the team – Kurt was going to be an exceptional father someday.

In between spending their weekdays in a classroom and their afternoons twice a week at Rutherford Park, the teens kept up with their homework assignments, term papers and book reports, plus my Saturday morning Shakespeare classes. Recently, fund-raising for the trip was added to their list of activities.

The SOS made serious plans to squeeze as much money as possible out of the residents of Fairfax County. Their parents had decided that it would be up to the teens to earn their own spending money for the trip.

"Car washes," said Kaija. "My dad's office is near a gas station on Duke Street and he said that they would let us wash cars there any time we want."

Raised eyebrow. "Which day? You people are running faster than hamsters on wheels as it is right now. Speaking of fund raising, need I remind you that Shakespeare's Birthday celebration at the Folger Shakespeare Library is next Saturday? No classes that day. If any of you want to dress up like Shakespeare's characters and come into Washington, DC, you have to be at the Folger by 9:30, bright and early Saturday morning."

For the past four years, I had taken volunteers from my classes to the Folger to help work at the William Shakespeare Birthday Fun Fair held on the lawn in front of the Library on the Saturday closest to April 23rd. The day was always well-attended by the general public. This year, the SOS would be allowed to sell balloons, face paint and work at the Make-A-Brooch Craft stall – all proceeds split among the helpers for their trip to Great Britain.

Hand in the air.

"Yes, Elizabeth?"

"Well, Kaija and I have an idea about that."

"Okay, what is it?" Brace yourself, it could be anything.

Elizabeth grinned. "Can we sell gingerbread Shakesbears?"

Cheers of agreement. Elizabeth had debuted her Shakesbears at the Christmas party last December and they were an instant hit. Shakesbears were gingerbread cookies made with a teddy bear cookie cutter and decorated with a sugar icing ruff, crown and striped gown for the Queen Elizabeth bear, and a ruff and striped, puffy pants for the Shakesbears. The thought of turning any kitchen over to Kaija and Elizabeth for the baking and decorating was a little daunting, but that could be more of a problem for Elizabeth's mother.

"I should think so. Just make sure each bear is packaged in its own baggie."

"Need help?" Kurt asked. "I could lick the bowls."

Both girls shouted an emphatic "No!"

"Can we do some car washes, too? " Kaija asked again.

"Okay, people, how many of you would be willing to wash cars? HAMLET will be over the first week in May. You can wash cars on Saturdays after that. All in favor, raise your hands."

Most of the team raised their hands.

"How about a yard sale?" Kathy suggested.

"Would you want to set that up?"

"Sure. Terri and Molly can help me."

"Okay, okay, folks. Listen up. Next Saturday, Shakespeare's Birthday at 9:30 AM. Then, after that, we will have about two months to do some car washes and a yard sale. I suggest you start planning on those now."

The level of noise rose accordingly. Nick yawned.

"I'm afraid can't help out. I'm the lead in the Spring play at school. It's my last year. The play will be up the weekend of May 14th. I can't do anything until after that. Oh, then there's Senior Prom, the Senior Spring

Follies, Junior-Senior Ring Breakfast, plus I've got a part-time job at the Blackeyed Pea Restaurant."

"Okay, okay, Nick, I get it. We'll see you in July."

He looked relieved. "Thank you."

"Just don't miss the plane."

Hand in the air.

"Yes, Kym?"

"We could charge admission for HAMLET."

"Kym, your parents will be coming to see you in HAMLET. They are also paying a thousand dollars to get you to England and back. I don't think it would be a good idea to charge them for HAMLET."

"When are we going to start playing a real cricket game?" Kurt wanted to know.

"Next Tuesday, so be on time, everyone."

Cheers and applause.

Hand in the air.

"Yes, Meaghan?" Meaghan Parker was Keene's older sister by a year. The Parkers were the only siblings on the team and they usually stayed as far away from each other as possible.

"Do you know where we will be playing in England?"

"Working on that."

Actually, things seemed to be moving along in England. While Zen and the other girls waited eagerly to hear from Eton, Bill Drake, the president of the Deddington Cricket Club, offered his cricket field. He had quickly responded to John and Carol Bassette's request for more cricket balls, and he had sent us two almost by return mail. A man who lived and dreamed cricket, Bill was more than anxious to host our neophyte team, and I had gratefully accepted his kind offer. If Eton College also agreed to host us, the SOS would have a real cricket tour in the United Kingdom. The

Deddington Cricketers would be older than the SOS, but the experience of playing a real team would be priceless.

Hand in the air.

"Yes, Elizabeth?"

"My parents want to know if we are going to play a cricket game here before we go. They want to see us."

Hadn't thought of that. "Working on it."

Actually, the team hadn't learned the rules or Laws for a real game as yet, but on a beautiful spring day in late April, Johnathon gathered everyone at the picnic table after their warm-up laps.

"Okay, folks, you know how to catch the ball pretty well now, and you know how to throw the ball and how to bat the ball. So now it's time to learn how to play this game."

"What's to learn?" Amy asked. "You hit the ball, then run to make a score."

Johnathon kept a straight face. "Sort of, but remember, cricket is not like baseball. There are no bases. You run to the opposite wicket and then you pop the crease."

Total silence for about thirty seconds.

"So, what's a crease?" Kurt asked.

"I'll tell you in a minute." Johnathon waved to everyone to sit on the grass in the shade. "Okay, this is the game of cricket," he began in a solemn tone. "And in cricket, almost anything goes."

Six hands waved in the air. Johnathon ignored them. "Moving on. To start the game – any game – the team captains toss a coin in the air to see which side goes first."

"Like baseball," someone whispered aloud.

Johnathon glared at the offending remark. "Never say cricket and baseball in the same breath. They aren't even kissing cousins. Now you all know the fielding positions –"

"Get your silly mid off my gully!" Muffled laughter.

"Zen!"

"Okay!" she yelled. "Sorry!"

Johnathon pushed his glasses up the bridge of his nose. "Today I'm talking about actually playing a game. After the coin toss, one team takes the fielding positions and the other team bats."

"Like baseball, " someone dared to whisper aloud.

Johnathon growled at the offender, then hurried on. "In baseball, you have one batter at home plate to start. In cricket, you always have two batsmen on the pitch – one in front of each wicket."

"Why?" Ellen asked.

Johnathon lifted one eyebrow. "Hold that thought. I'll answer you in a minute." He cleared this throat. "Also on the field are two umpires, usually one at each wicket. Everyone got that so far?"

"So, then what?" Kurt asked.

"Okay, one batsman gets ready for the throw while the other batsman gets ready to run."

"What?" Katie asked, wrinkling her nose. "I thought the one that hits the ball runs."

"He does. The bowler throws the ball at the first batter. Batter hits the ball to kingdom come and both batsmen run."

"Where?" Carol asked.

Johnathon took a deep breath. "To the opposite wicket. The batsmen pass one another, back and forth, in the middle of the pitch."

"Where they High Five each other," Zen added. More laughter.

"That's crazy," Steve muttered under his breath.

"No, that's cricket. Moving along – now, the batsman, who is up, has several choices –"

"Three strikes and you're out!" Kaija cheered.

Johnathon kept his cool. "No way. To begin with, the batter doesn't even have to hit the ball. He or she can just stand there and let the ball go by."

"Like a ball, in baseball," Kurt observed to Carol who was sitting next to him.

Johnathon took another deep breath. "More or less, except they are not called balls, they are call 'leaves' and the batter can have as many balls or leaves as he or she wants as long as the ball doesn't hit the wicket and knock off the bails."

"The what?" Julie asked.

"Those thingies on top of the wicket," Terri told her.

"And if the wicket is broken –" Johnathon continued.

"The game is over!"

"Zen!"

"Sorry," said the grinning unrepentant.

Johnathon gripped his notebook tighter. "If the wicket is broken by the ball, then the batsman who is up is now out. That's called being bowled out. It's one of six ways for a batsman to be out."

"Six!" Keene groaned and flopped on his back. "We're never going to remember all this stuff."

"Look at it this way, folks, if anything happens to the wicket, the batter is out. Okay, let's get back to the batsmen. Say he or she hits the ball, then both batters run to the opposite wickets. That's one run –"

"That's two runs," Kurt protested. "Two batters at two wickets, both running. That's two runs."

Johnathon shook his head. "Sorry, not in this game. Only one run. Only the batsman that hit the ball is the one who scores. Unless, of course, the ball has gone so far out of the field, the batter will have time enough to run back across the pitch, making two runs."

"So, what does the other batter do?"

"Pays attention and runs when the first batter tells him or her to run."

Hand in the air – for once.

"Yes, Kurt?"

"What's a home run? Does cricket have a homer?"

Johnathon nodded. "The answer is yes, if the two batters can run back and forth for six consecutive times, then that is a home run. The trick is to know when to stop running."

Jamie raised his hand. "Okay, the batters can change ends. That way each batter gets a chance to rest. Right?"

"Not exactly – because the bowlers also change ends."

Keene sat upright. "What? That's crazy. It sounds like something straight out of 'Alice in Wonderland.' "

Johnathon chuckled. "That's cricket. Now listen up, people. The bowler –"

"Meaning the pitcher," said Kurt to Carol.

"Wait!" The Mighty Mite stood up so that Johnathon could see her. "Wait a minute, please. Let me get this straight. The batters change sides, does that mean that the bowlers also shift around too?"

Johnathon nodded. "Exactly. You got it."

"What?" Kurt yelled.

Johnathon took a deep breath. "Just as there are two batters and two umpires at each wicket, there are also two bowlers. One does the pitching, while the other one fields behind the opposite wicket. Then, after the first bowler throws six good balls, meaning no fouls, the umpire shouts 'over,' and second bowler throws the ball by his wicket, and the first bowler fields behind the first wicket."

"Why?" Susan asked.

Their coach just shrugged his shoulders. "Who knows? Look, people, I'm not making any of this stuff up. It's all in the Book of Laws." He waved the rule book.

Another hand in the air.

"Yes, Molly?"

"And the batters?"

"They stay put. They don't move until the ball is in play again."

Molly rubbed her nose. "And then they run back and forth? When do they stop?"

"When the wicket keeper has the ball in her hand."

Jamie cleared his throat. "Not the pitcher, er, bowler?"

Johnathon shook his head and glanced at his watch. Precious practice time was flying away. "Nope. It's the wicket keeper. At that point, the ball is considered dead."

"Then what?" Kathy asked.

"Then the wicket keeper throws the ball to the bowler and the whole routine starts all over again."

"So, what's an out?" Kurt wanted to know. "You said the batter is out if the bowler hits the wicket. What else is an out?"

Johnathon managed a brief smile. "Glad you asked that question, Kurt. There are six kinds of outs. We've just been talking about the bowled out. Then there's the caught out – that's like a flyball."

Keene leaned over to Steve and mumbled, "That's the first thing I've heard today that makes sense."

"Then there's something called stumped out –"

Kym arched her eyebrow. "Like when the batter is too stupid to hit a good ball?"

Johnathon sighed. "No, Kym, it means that the batter has moved out of his box – his crease – when the wicket keeper catches the ball."

Hand in the air. "What did you say a crease was?" Amy wanted to know.

Johnathon pushed his glasses back up the bridge of his nose again. "The crease lines mark a rectangle at each wicket. You know, where we put out the cones? The batting crease marks how far the batsmen can move toward the bowler. If any of you steps beyond that crease mark when you are swinging the bat, the umpire will call 'stumped' and you are out. It has nothing to do with hitting the wicket."

"Even if the batter hits the ball?" Amy persisted.

"Yep." Johnathon glanced at his watch again. "Moving on, folks. The batsman can also be out if he or she accidently knocks over the wicket on the back swing. That's called a 'hit wicket out.' "

"Cripes!" someone moaned. "A sticky hit wicket."

Johnathon ignored the remark. "And if the batters are running between the wickets, but the striker doesn't reach the opposite wicket before the keeper gets the ball, that's called a run out."

"Okay, " said Kurt. "That's five ways to get out. What's the sixth?"

Their coach sighed. "Yeah, I was just coming to that one. It's something called Leg Before the Wicket, and to be honest, I really don't understand what it means. Don't worry about it. If the ump calls you're out, don't argue. You're out. That, boys and girls, is cricket. Any questions? Yes, Ellen?"

"Can we play now?"

Teri Anderson and another SOS team member help to buckle Susan Linsert into her batter's pads. (Linsert Family Collection)

CHAPTER FIVE

May 1988

"As full of spirit as the month of May"

Henry IV, Part 1

The merry month of May arrived at Rutherford Park's cricket field. With the final performance of HAMLET behind them, there was nothing to distract the SOS Cricket Team, except their schools' standardized tests, lost library books, and thoughts of the upcoming trip to England in July. As the weather grew drier and hotter, the team's expertise in the game got better. A second set of wickets, bat and ball was donated to the team by friends of Keene and Meaghan's family. Now the SOS had a proper pitch with a wicket at each end and two bats for the strikers. With three balls now at hand, there was less concern over the loss of one, which happened one humid afternoon, when the oldest ball flew past Amy and Steve, both of whom were playing the Long Leg position in the effort to keep the ball away from the baseball field. It landed somewhere deep into the poison ivy-shrouded woods. Steve dashed after it, while the rest of the team froze in place, except the batsmen, who happily ran back and forth between the wickets for six runs. Meanwhile, Steve thrashed around in the woods out of sight.

Note to self: warn Mrs. Fender that Steve will probably have poison ivy blisters by nightfall.

Steve finally returned, but without the ball.

"No problem," Johnathon yelled across the pitch where he was acting as umpire. "Rinse your hands, then drink some water. Okay, next batter up!"

Mary W. Schaller

Both the score keepers, Julie and Kym, were now making notes on batting positions, number of wickets hit, number of runs made and by whom, but as of yet, neither of them had ever seen an official cricket score sheet. Everyone thought it was the same as a baseball one. They were in for a surprise.

Since the team was shaping up so well, it was time to give them a little publicity, just as we did for the Shakespeare plays. One Monday afternoon, while the kids were living their real lives outside of Shakespeare and cricket practice, I put together a press kit that introduced the SOS team, why and where the team were practicing and the kids' goal to meet English boys and girls on a cricket field. Without a second thought, I mailed off copies to the Sports Editors of the Washington POST, and the Washington TIMES, as well as to the local Fairfax JOURNAL and the Fairfax CONNECTION. I had expected that the CONNECTION, Fairfax's lesser weekly news sheet, would contact me.

It didn't. On the other hand, both the JOURNAL and the TIMES did. Two out of four was unbelievable – especially since the TIMES was the second largest newspaper in the Washington Metropolitan area. Both editors wanted to send out reporters -- and photographers -- in early June.

The team needed to get their tee shirts cleaned!

Back in early April, two of the SOS girls had created a logo for the team that was both tasteful and professional-looking. The letters S O S were superimposed over a simple compass rose that pointed the four directions. The words "Shakespeareans OverSeas" encircled the compass. Bill, Fairfax County's favorite tee shirt silk screener who worked out of his bachelor pad in Fairfax City, complimented this design as being better than our usual Shakespeare ones from past years. In addition to the black tee shirts, he not only screened the logo onto the team's personal duffle bags, but he also added black baseball caps for free. With the kids in their white pants, the black tees and the ball caps, they were going to look very professional.

60

The Most Improbable International Cricket Team Ever: A True Story

At the late April Cultural Sunday meeting, there was the predictable noise, squeals, and cheers over the shirts and the bags, especially since each member had his or her name embroidered on their duffle. But revolution erupted over the ball caps.

"Do we have to wear these hats?" Kym wrinkled her nose.

"It's the team hat. You are a member of the team. You wear the hat."

"It looks stupid," remarked our fashionista, Sabrina.

"The other team will be very impressed."

"Not if the other team is Eton." Zen curled her lip.

"The crown sits too high," Kaija pointed out. "It'll make me look like I have a swelled head."

One of the boys muttered something uncomplimentary.

"I'm not wearing this," Julie said emphatically.

"I like it," Kurt announced to the room in general.

"I like it," echoed Paul. He put on his cap and beamed. It meant more to him than any of the others realized.

Nick just laughed and twirled his hat around his finger. It would be a cold day in Hell before he would wear the team cap, though it didn't matter because Nick didn't intend to play out on the field.

I ignored the general uprising. "Please wear your tee shirts to the Folger for Shakespeare's Birthday, if you don't plan on wearing your costumes."

The Battle of the Ballcaps could wait another day.

At the Folger Shakespeare Library's Birthday celebration, most of the team wore their costumes because, being actors at heart, they loved to wear costumes. A few did opt for the tee shirts. It was gratifying to hear the compliments from some of the Folger staff over the shirt's design. It really did look sharp.

Now, a few weeks later, the tee shirts would make their official debut for the Press.

An avalanche of noise greeted the announcement of the reporters' visits.

"You mean we're going to be interviewed?" Meaghan asked. "Like in a newspaper?"

"Why?" Kathy asked.

"Because you people are doing something unusual. You're learning to play cricket so that you can go to England in July and play a game over there. It means, folks, that you are going to be a real international sports team representing the United States of America."

Dead silence in the room, for once.

"Wow!" whispered Keene.

"I had no idea what cricket was about when we started it," said Carol later explained, "so I really didn't think whether it was unique that we were doing it."

"Okay, people, we are expecting the reporter to come to Rutherford Park on June 10th. I want all of you there as early as possible with clean shirts, clean pants . . . and your ballcaps."

On Friday, June 10th most of the team showed up at Rutherford Park in their white pants, black tee shirts and ballcaps. Most of them did not wear their ballcaps, except for Molly – who wore a red one.

"Molly! Where's your SOS cap?"

"You just said to wear a ballcap, so I'm wearing mine." Not for nothing was her nickname "Impy."

Pretend that the ballcaps are not an issue.

"Okay, people, run! Two laps!"

"That will get our shirts all sweaty," Julie whined.

"Then you'll look authentic. Two laps, please!"

The Most Improbable International Cricket Team Ever: A True Story

The reporter from the Washington TIMES, Gary Graves, arrived accompanied by the paper's photographer, Tracy Woodward. The SOS team beamed. The girls preened. Kurt and Paul adjusted their team ballcaps.

For the next hour Mr. Graves interviewed the kids while Ms. Woodward took a number of pictures of Johnathon working with individual team members. The reporter seemed much impressed by the kids' knowledge of cricket. He was even more surprised when he hefted one of the balls.

"Any of you ever been hit by one of these?"

Everyone nodded. A bruise from the cricket ball was considered a badge of honor.

He was equally impressed by the bowlers, especially when little Susan backed up for her first run.

"Does she really pitch?" he asked.

"Yep," replied Steve, as Susan charged up to the bowling crease and hurled the ball down the pitch to Amy. The ball bounced just offside of Amy, then the wicket exploded behind her. Terri, the wicket keeper, deftly scooped up the ball and threw it back to Susan.

"That's Susan. We call her the Mighty Mite," Steve said in an offhand manner, clearly proud of the team's youngest member. Mr. Graves whistled under his breath, and he jotted down several more notes.

"You've got a great bunch of kids here," the reporter told me before leaving. "When you get back, call me and let me know what the score was in England."

On the following Tuesday, Robert Bell, the reporter from the Fairfax JOURNAL came to watch the SOS practice. He, too, was accompanied by a photographer, Cheryl Reed. Once again the team wore their freshly laundered white pants and team shirts. Only Kurt and Paul wore their caps. Molly again had her red hat and a cocky grin.

The team rose to the occasion. They acted and sounded professional, as if they had been playing cricket all their lives, instead of only the past two months. The team was definitely coming together as one group, instead of several dozen individuals. Terri was especially proud. "I loved our teamwork and the chance to bond in a different way," she said.

"How do you think you'll do when you play cricket in England?" Mr. Bell asked.

"We'll probably get killed," Jamie replied with a grin. "We're a lot better than when we started, but those teams in England have been playing for a long time. We won't be terrible, though, and we'll have a good time playing them."

The TIMES's article came out on June 15th. The team was thrilled by the two-column story, especially Susan. It was obvious that she had charmed and amazed Mr. Graves.

"The best bowler, so far, is the youngest and smallest, 13-year-old Susan Linsert," he wrote. "Called the 'Mighty Mite' because of her size [4 feet 10] she keeps most of her bowls inside the batsman's box and has been known to shatter a wicket or two."

Team parents snapped up extra copies of the TIMES. The publicity gave the SOS the boost of confidence they needed. However, the kids were a bit disappointed that their photos did not appear in the paper – except for Molly. There she was, in her white baggy shorts, her SOS tee shirt -- and her red ballcap -- in living color on the front page of the TIMES Sports section.

The following day, my phone rang.

"Good morning, Mrs. Schaller, this is Dave Keegan," he said in an English accent of sorts. "I saw the article about your team in the Washington TIMES."

Surprised. "Good morning, what can I do for you?"

"I'm the president of the Massachusetts Avenue Cricket Club, and I would very much like to come out to one of your practices and watch your team play. I've never heard of any youth cricket team in the area. Perhaps I may be of some help."

Oh, wow!

Dave Keegan was more than "some help." He was a godsend. He had a job with the New Zealand Embassy in Washington, but his passion was cricket. Seeing the photo of Johnathon trying to get Molly's arm into the proper bowling position was enough to convince Mr. Keegan that we were in trouble.

Though why was Johnathon showing Molly how to bowl when Molly preferred to play the Gully position?

"That was the photographer's idea. It was the red hat," Johnathon explained at the next practice. Being a part-time photographer himself, he had a point. Black and white uniforms don't photograph in color as well as something bright red. Maybe our Impy was on to a good thing.

Mr. Keegan arrived and once the team heard his Kiwi accent, he had their undivided attention. They were very impressed that a real cricketeer from a foreign country had come all the way out to Fairfax from Washington just to watch them play. They gave their best practice that hot afternoon.

Standing next to me on the sidelines, Mr. Keegan winced when he saw Terri take her place behind the wicket. "Where are her pads?" he asked.

"What pads?"

"Padding. The wicketkeeper should be wearing pads on her legs and she needs keeper's gloves."

"We don't have anything like that. We had a tough enough time just getting a wicket, a bat and a few balls. And we've already lost one ball as it is. I'm holding my breath for the other two."

At that point, Kathy came on the field with the bat.

"My God, no pads for the batsman either?"

With growing guilt. "No, I'm afraid not. We didn't know about pads. And I don't think we can get any around here."

Mr. Keegan gave a little shudder, then turned his attention to the bowling as Keene began his first run.

The rest of that afternoon was taken up with the finer points of bowling position and proper batsman stance. Mr. Keegan complimented the bowlers, the batters and the fielders, especially for their ability to keep the ball from hitting the creek, the passing cars, and the baseball players in the next field. At the end of the practice, Mr. Keegan thanked the team, and their coach. Then he said,

"Next time I come, I'll bring you some pads. They can't keep on playing without pads." With that, he hurried to his car, and drove back to Washington in the full evening rush hour traffic.

"That was awesome!" the bowlers said.

"He's cool," the batters and fielders said.

"He's just what we needed," Johnathon said. "I never knew half that stuff he was telling the bowlers."

Stunned. "I feel like we've just been visited by the cricket version of the fairy godfather."

That evening, the telephone rang. "Hello, Mrs. Schaller? Are you the lady with the cricket team?"

The caller was Mr. Fazil Karim, a Pakistani gentleman, who was the President of the Metro Sports Club, another one of the diplomatic teams that held weekly cricket matches on the playing fields near the State Department in downtown Washington. He, too, had read about the SOS in the Washington TIMES newspaper and he wanted to visit the team at practice.

Events were taking a decidedly international flavor.

"Bring him on," said Johnathon when I told him of our latest admirer. "The more the merrier."

The following Monday, the Fairfax JOURNAL printed their story of the SOS cricket team under the headline, "Cricket Finds Fans in No. VA."

"Yes, cricket," the article began. " The prim and proper sport of England has been somewhat Americanized by a group of Fairfax County teenagers, trying to, if not mastering the game, then at least understand it."

The article went on for three columns on the front page of the Sports section, but only one photograph – of Johnathon hitting a ball. He looked a little sheepish when the SOS confronted him.

"The photographer was a nice lady. She asked me to demonstrate batting practice. So I did."

Despite no team pictures, the article did wonders for the kids' reputations at their various schools around the county. Suddenly, being a cricketeer was cool. Even the baseball players on the field next door to us took the time to come over and actually watch what the SOS were doing on their measly piece of waste ground. The girls didn't mind a bit.

Kathy Robinson misses the ball. Wicket keeper Terri Anderson waits to catch it.

(Paul Miller)

Mr. Karim came to the next practice, wearing an all- white cricket uniform. He was polite, soft-spoken and very professional. While Dave Keegan had been more interested in the bowling, Mr. Karim gave most of his attention to the batsmen. He didn't say a thing about pads.

"You have score keepers?" he asked. In cricket, each team usually has two score keepers.

"Yes, we do. Kym and Julie."

He looked over to where the two girls sat under the shade of a tree. Both held spiral notebooks in their hands. Mr. Karim ambled over to them, and engaged the girls in deep conversation.

At the end of the day's practice, Mr. Karim complimented the team. Then he invited everyone to come watch his team play in Washington on the upcoming Saturday. "It would be our pleasure to host you."

"We'd love to come," said Kathy, speaking for the team before Johnathon could say a word.

"Two o'clock," Mr. Karim said. The he touched the brim of his cap and left.

"Wow," breathed Kym. "We've been keeping score all wrong! And Mr. Karim promised to bring us real score sheets next time."

Julie just looked stunned.

That evening, the telephone rang. My husband, Marty, answered it. Then he looked at me. "It's for you. This guy has a British accent."

Must be Dave Keegan.

No, it was Mr. Peter Rogers of Portsmouth, England. A homesick Brit, he had seen our article in the JOURNAL, and he politely asked if he could come to watch us play.

Of course, he could! The SOS Cricket Team's company of advisors was getting more global by the hour.

Two days later, Kathy, Keene, Kym, Zen, Carol, Jamie and a few others piled into several cars and we drove into Washington to the playing fields in West Potomac Park in Washington, DC. Johnathon had to work, though he would have loved to join the group. Fortunately, on-street parking in downtown Washington was easy to find on a hot Saturday afternoon in June. Fazil Karim seemed delighted that the SOS actually showed up as he introduced the team to his cricketeers, all of whom were dressed in pure whites. The SOS dressed mostly in their team shirts and shorts. Keene actually wore his ballcap. Fazil seated the group on the park's only bleacher under the only tree on the field. Then he dashed back to his game, which SOS's arrival had interrupted.

Watching a real game was highly instructive. It was the first time the kids had seen how the players used the two sets of wickets. Nor had the SOS really understood why the players ran with the bat, instead of dropping it like they do in baseball, until they saw the game in action. The bowling looked lethal.

"Wow! How fast was that ball going?" Keene asked Jamie after witnessing a particularly ferocious pitch.

Jamie shook his head. "Faster than we throw, that's for sure."

"You know, you could get killed that way," Carol said with a touch of awe in her voice.

"I see what Mr. Keegan means by padding," Zen added, as a player was hit in the shin by a ball.

Thank heavens he promised he would bring us some!

Just then two or three of the batsmen yelled out something like "hozat", and the game stopped while everyone threw up their hands and started shouting at the umpire.

"What just happened?" Kathy asked, but none of us could figure it out.

"They sound just like us sometimes," Carol observed as the noise around the umpire increased a notch.

"We'll ask Mr. Karim whenever he comes over here."

The umpire stood his ground amid the torrent of words, then raised one finger in the air. At that, everyone shut up, and returned to their original positions. The bowler hurled another fireball down the pitch.

After watching about forty minutes of play, the SOS members began to wilt in the late May heat and humidity despite the shade and the water they had brought with them. We had just about decided to slip away, when the umpire called for a time out, and all the players ran for the row of coolers. Fazil came up to us with a big smile.

"What do you think?"

"Interesting," said Kathy. "But we didn't understand what happened when everyone stopped and yelled at the umpire."

Fazil laughed softly. "Did you hear them shout 'Howzat?," he asked with a twinkle in his eye.

The kids nodded.

"The batting team was appealing the umpire to reconsider his ruling on that last batsman. They shout 'Howzat', meaning 'How is that?' They were asking if the batsman was really out."

"And was he?" Zen asked.

"Oh, my, yes. It was a definite case of Leg Before the Wicket."

Johnathon had puzzled over this particular term when he encountered it in the Book of Laws, but he couldn't understand exactly what it meant. On this afternoon, it was far too hot to ask for an explanation. The SOS was ready to scamper back to the air-conditioned cars, go back to Fairfax County and hit the McDonald's for burgers. The team was never happier than when eating.

"I shall come see you next week, yes?" Fazil asked by way of a farewell.

Yes, please!

Once in the car, with the air conditioning on full blast, Jamie remarked, "We're going to get killed in England."

Jamie Fox bowls while Zen Mason waits to run down the pitch at the Exhibition Game. (Johnathon Bigelow)

Mary W. Schaller

The SOS Exhibition Game

Burke Garden Center, Burke, Virginia

JUNE 25, 1988

Kurt Bose bowls while Kathy Robinson waits for her partner to make a hit. Katie
Shirly fields in the Mid Off position. Fazil Karim, President of the {Washington,
DC} Metro Sports Club umpires. (Johnathon Bigelow)

CHAPTER SIX

June 1988

"Bid the players make haste."

Hamlet

Suddenly, it was the middle of June. In three more weeks, the SOS would be airborne and on the way across the Atlantic to England. Events accelerated. Nick graduated from high school, and he was already looking toward August when he would move into his dorm at James Madison University in southwestern Virginia. Becky was liberated from her school in Connecticut and she was glad to be back with the team again. Ellen and Susan both celebrated their momentous 13th birthdays that now ushered them into the official teenage years. And Zen had finally heard from Eton College.

No one was interested in doing the warmup laps. Everyone wanted to see the envelope that she waved.

Heart pounding. "So, what did Eton say?"

"Sadly, they said no. They said that the boys will be out of school for their summer holidays and the school will be closed."

Internal sigh of relief.

Loud moan from the girls.

"Who died?" Johnathon asked when he arrived on the field. "Why aren't you guys running?"

"Eton said no," Angela pouted.

"Good," said Kurt. "Those guys are probably a bunch of snobs anyway."

Zen caressed the envelope that had a gothic-looking seal on the flap. "Can I keep the letter?" she asked. Zen didn't strike one as the sentimental type, but then again, she was always full of unexpected surprises.

"Sure, you wrote to them. You can keep the reply."

"So, who are we going to play?" asked Meaghan.

Clearing throat. "Well, Mr. Drake of the Deddington Cricket Club is getting us a team. He has promised it will be just what we want."

"We wanted Eton," Zen mumbled.

"Are we going to play a game here before we go?" Elizabeth asked again as she had done at almost every practice for a month.

"Yes! As a matter of fact, I was just about to announce that we will be doing a special Exhibition Game a week from Saturday."

"Where?"

"What time?

"Can anyone come?"

The School of Experience had taught me never to rely on the spoken word when giving out important information. Kathy took my stack of fliers that announced the Game and passed them out to everyone who was present at practice.

"The Burke Garden Center? Will we be playing around the flower beds?"

"No, they have a large grassy field at one end, and Mr. Ron DeAngeles, who owns the Garden Center, says he will advertise our game on their announcement board."

The usual noise bubbled over.

"Who are we going to play?"

"Johnathon will divide you up on game day. You all know how to field and how to bat. We have two scorekeepers, four bowlers and two wicket keepers, so we will have enough for two teams. And you will also notice on the flier that we want you at the Garden Center by 6:30 PM, wearing your SOS shirts, white pants – and ballcaps. We are going to be taking the official team photograph then."

Johnathon raised his hand. Instant silence.

"And one more thing, people. You need to elect your team captains at the next practice. To be fair, there should be one boy and one girl who will be the SOS Team co-captains, so you have the weekend to think about it. They will be your captains for the game here and the game in England."

Instant hubbub. Johnathon allowed them five minutes of loud discussion, before blowing his whistle. "Okay, now, RUN!"

After three months of running around the field, the SOS finished their two laps in record time. "All right, folks," Jonathon continued, "Terri, you are wicket-keeper for the first over. Keene, you're bowling the first over. Jamie, you're up for the second over. Kathy, you're first batsman. Kurt, you're second. You'll partner each other. Remember about partnering?"

"Saw it last Saturday," Kathy shouted back as she grabbed one of the bats.

"Hey, batter, batter, batter, batter, swing!" Kurt yelled encouragement.

"Hey! Look!," shouted Julie, pointing toward the parking lot. "It's Mr. Keegan and he's got a big bag of stuff!"

Pads?

Instantly, the SOS surrounded Dave. First, he handed out the wicket keeper's set, which Terri grabbed before Kaija could get them. The two girls retreated off to one side to figure out how to put on the high leg protectors and the huge, thick gloves. Meanwhile, Dave extracted a second set of long pads.

"These are for the batsmen."

"That's me." Kathy stepped forward. "I'm first up." She picked up one of the leg protectors, saw all the buckles in the back and turned to Zen. "Can you help me with these, please?"

Mary W. Schaller

Once Terri was buckled into her keeper's set, she took a step and started to laugh. "How do we walk in these things?" The leg pads went up to her mid-thigh. She wagged her hands, now encased in the over-size padded gloves. "I'll be lucky to hold anything with these on." She duck-walked to her place behind the wicket. "Come on, Kathy!" She yelled.

Kathy was having just as much trouble with her leg pads. Like Terri's set, her pads came up to mid-thigh. Then she pulled on the batsman's gloves which were not as thick as Terri's, but still large. She took a wide-swinging walk to the batsman's position. "Okay, Keene," she shouted to the bowler. "Let's give it a try."

The rest of the team scattered around the field as Keene began his run. Kathy hit the ball squarely. It flew off toward the creek where Steve and Molly were waiting to catch it.

"Run, Kathy!" Johnathon yelled, trying to keep a straight face. Kathy attempted a wide-swinging stride.

"This is impossible!" she said as she nearly lost her balance.

Dave grinned "I'd say they need a bit of practice."

Actually, the kids needed wings and a prayer.

Meanwhile, Terri seemed rooted to her spot when Steve returned the ball. "I'm having trouble moving sideways!"

When Keene bowled again, the ball flew past Terri out of reach. Katie, behind her, caught it before it sailed into the woods. Terri shuffled over Katie and retrieved the ball.

"Can I bat again?" Kathy asked. "I think I can get it."

Keene trotted back for his run. Kathy held onto the bat with a look of grim determination on her face. Terri crouched down behind the wicket. Keene bowled and Kathy hit it again. This time she headed down the pitch to the opposite wicket with a gait that was a cross between a penguin waddle and a bunny hop.

"Don't laugh!" she yelled at her teammates, who were giggling. "Just you wait until you wear these things."

"Kurt, batter up!" Johnathon yelled, as Kathy unbuckled the padding.

Because he was taller and because he would rather die than look like an idiot, Kurt managed to swagger up to the batsman's crease wearing the pads. "Okay, Keene! Let 'er rip!"

Keene did. Kurt took a swing, missed and almost fell backward. Terri did a few hops and sideways shuffle to retrieve the ball, but, at least, she was moving better than before.

"Can I try that again?" Kurt yelled.

"Next batter!" Johnathon called.

For the rest of the practice, every member of the team had the experience of wearing the pads while running, except for Paul, who laughed, and said he'd rather take their pictures instead.

Keene, Steve and Jamie didn't have too much trouble with the leg pads as these three boys were all nearly six feet tall. After a lot of starts and falls, most of the girls as well as Kurt could manage a trot. Predictably, the youngest members, Carol, Ellen and Susan, encountered the most trouble. The pads nearly came up to their waists.

"There is no way I can do this," said Ellen, wrinkling her nose. She hopped over to Susan. "You try."

With the help of Katie and Carol, Ellen was freed of the pads and she watched as the girls buckled up the Mighty Mite. "Take small steps, Susan," Ellen advised.

Susan stood still for a moment as she shifted her weight back and forth. Then she went into a small crouch and managed a bit of a run before tumbling onto the grass. "I'll get it!" she yelled as Kym and Angela helped her back upright.

At last, Dave looked at his watch, decided that it was time for him to play in the rush hour traffic, and, with a cheery "Good luck," he left. He passed a new visitor who had just arrived on the field.

"Who's that, I wonder?" Johnathon said in an aside.

"I think he's the guy from England."

"Hope he has a sense of humor."

Peter Rogers was a jolly, charming Englishmen. The team immediately warmed to him. He gave them a few helpful pointers about running in the pads, then he settled back to watch the team play. He was a life-long fan of cricket and had missed seeing his favorite sport when he moved to the States after marrying his American wife. He didn't belong to any cricket club because he lived in Fairfax and getting to the teams in Washington was difficult. He was absolutely thrilled that there was a cricket team nearby.

Watching the SOS players switch pads with the next batter, he remarked, "You know, they are going to have to learn to do that faster. There's a cricket Law that will penalize you if the next batsman doesn't get to the pitch quickly."

"What?" Johnathon pulled out his well-worn copy of the Cricket Laws. "Where?" The two men got into a huddle over the book until the appropriate rule had been located. "Law 31, an incoming batsman shall be timed out, if he takes more than two minutes to come in." He looked up at Mr. Rogers, than at me.

"We're dead."

"No, we'll practice and do the changing in teams. Two people peel the pads off the first batter while two people start buckling the second batter into them."

Peter nodded. "Could work. Usually every batter has his own pads."

"We only have the one pair."

Helping each other in and out of the pads actually made the team closer knit, and it gave the extra fielders something to do. For the rest of the practice, every member had a chance to bat and run with the pads. Meanwhile, Johnathon timed everyone else as they made the switch. By the end of practice, most were able to get into the pads in two and a half minutes.

"Next time, we'll shave off those thirty seconds."

"I've got to cut my nails," mumbled Libby, nursing a split index fingernail.

A second letter from England lay on our dining room table when I got home from practice. Bill Drake regretted to inform me that our backup opponents at Deddington were going to be in Banbury playing an away game on the same day and time that we were going to be at the Deddington Cricket Club.

Heavy sinking feeling.

However – Bill planned to make an appeal for a co-ed team on the local radio station. He had high hopes for more players.

Went to bed with a headache.

The late afternoon of Saturday, June the 25th was perfect in every respect. Virginia's usual suffocating humidity was lower. So was the temperature. The bugs were at a minimum thanks to a refreshing breeze, and Ron DeAngeles of the Burke Garden Center had the grass mowed to a perfect height – no pebbles, no creek, no close woods and no baseball team nearby. In fact, it was the best ground that the team had ever played on. The sun hovered behind a stand of the tall trees that backed onto the Center, allowing the game to be played in the shade. A large American flag atop a tall, white pole flew majestically over the field, making the scene look like a professional sporting event. All the parents came, armed with lawn chairs, cameras and large hampers of food and drink. Since the Garden Center had a big parking lot, there was no problem for all the extra cars.

Fazil and Peter Rogers had graciously agreed to act as umpires, a blessing since the team would accept their rulings easier than anything

Johnathon said. Dave Keegan was unable to attend, but he donated a brand-new regulation cricket ball for the game. Appropriately, there was a golden New Zealand Kiwi stamped on it.

After several days of many phone calls among themselves, the team had finally chosen their co-captains. For the boys, it was Keene, one of the team's best all-around players. For the girls, it was Julie, who won the honor because, at the age of sixteen-and-a-half years old, she was the eldest girl on the team, beating out Zen by two weeks. Julie swelled with pride.

Just after six-thirty that evening, Johnathon gathered the team together for the group photo. That was the cue for a large number of proud fathers and mothers to pull out their cameras. For once, most of the twenty-four members of the SOS were on the playing field at the same time. Everyone on the team had dressed in their clean, black tee shirts and white pants – mostly shorts for both girls and boys since the evening was still very warm. As usual, Kurt was the only team member to wear his SOS ball cap. The kids looked good – and they knew it. It was the first time that the parents had seen the team together in full uniform. Since the photo shoot took place near the roadside fence, a lot of passing cars slowed down to gawk this unfamiliar co-ed group. Many of them honked approval. A few, seeing the Garden Center's sign advertising the cricket game, pulled into the lot and parked. The drivers asked what was going on.

"It's an exhibition game for the SOS Cricket team. They're going to England in two weeks to play at Oxford."

Some people remembered reading about the team in the JOURNAL. Several of the drivers asked, "May we stay and watch?"

"Of course! You can park right over there."

"I once saw cricket played in England, but I never expected to see it in Fairfax County," one man told us.

The SOS Team, aware that a sizable audience was building up, caught the excitement. Their spirits ran high. This was really IT!

Fazil and Peter arrived. Fazil again wore his regulation cricket uniform of all white pants , shirt and shoes. Peter was more comfortable in a polo shirt and shorts. As a thank you gift for the umpires, the team donated two black SOS ball caps to them. The gentlemen immediately put on the caps and seemed very pleased with their gifts. The team members were very happy to get rid of at least two more hats.

The boys set up the wickets and cones which aroused a lot of interest among the spectators. This certainly didn't look a thing like baseball. Johnathon tactfully asked some of the crowd to move back as their picnics were in the "outfield."

There was a short welcome speech to the audience, coupled with thanks to the two umpires and to Ron DeAngeles for the use of the field. Then followed a short explanation of what was going to happen. The teams were short-sided, meaning playing with less than the usual eleven fielders, and the game would be played with limited overs, meaning that the four bowlers would each throw two sets of six good "pitches". Kym took her position on the sideline with an official cricket scoresheet in hand, thanks to Fazil, who stood near her to help in case Kym got confused in the score keeping. Julie, now promoted to a co-captain, fielded in this game to even the number of players on each side. The game started with the traditional coin toss between Keene and Julie. Keene's side lost and Julie elected to bat.

Terri, as first wicket keeper, donned her pads and took her position behind the nearside wicket. Kaija, the other keeper, was on the opposite team and she stood in line to bat. Jamie, the first bowler, loosened up on the far end of the pitch while he waited for the game to begin. The audience leaned forward in their seats, waiting to see what would happen next. Most of them had never seen a cricket match before this evening, and they knew very little about the game. After the signal from Fazil that the teams looked ready to play, the whistle blew, and play commenced.

My heart swelled with pride, watching the kids bowl, bat, catch, run and have the time of their lives. In four short months, the ragtag SOS had come a long, long way from having no equipment and no idea how to play cricket into this smoothly working team, who now demonstrated their new expertise. The parents may have wondered what was happening and who was winning, but those concerns were incidental to the players. The SOS were bowling, batting and fielding well, and they knew it. The kids took pleasure in doing something that most of their contemporaries in Fairfax County knew nothing about.

Unlike almost every other sport on the face of the earth, cricket teams who play on Sunday afternoons on English village greens don't worry very much about who wins the game. To ask an Englishman who is winning is considered almost an insult. As a matter of fact, most cricket games end in a draw – and no one minds that very much. The talk around the pub following a beautiful, sunny afternoon of cricket will be about the brilliant batting done by young Jasper, or the astounding catch that good old Rupert made at the end of the fifth over. The bowler will be congratulated by the number of wickets he toppled. The actual score is immaterial.

On the other hand, the scores in test Matches and in First Class cricket matter very much indeed.

The great American sportswriter of the twentieth century, Grantland Rice [1880 – 1954], said it best when he coined the immortal phrase, "It's not whether you win or lose, it's how you play the game."

Cricket has traditionally been a game that requires not only skills in bowling and batting, but also the virtues of honesty, integrity, fair play and teamwork. Cricket teams play hard, but they play fair. Teams must respect their opponents, as well as respect the Laws of the game and the judgements of the umpires. People who don't are said to be "not cricket." The very name of the game has come to mean "straight" or "fair." That is the Spirit of Cricket.

Twelve years after the SOS hung up their bats and tee shirts, the Marylebone Cricket Club finally put into words the description of this elusive "Spirit" when the MCC added a Preamble to their Code of Laws. The

Preamble states that "Cricket owes much of its appeal and enjoyment to the fact that it should be played not only according to the Laws, but also within the Spirit of Cricket. The major responsibility for ensuring fair play rests with the captains, but extends to all players, match officials and, especially in junior cricket, teachers, coaches and parents. Respect is central to the Spirit of Cricket."

In short, most of the time, winning is beside the point in cricket. The SOS team sort of understood that, although most of their parents didn't get it at all. The adults were used to attending their children's soccer matches, Little League games, swim meets and football games where there is often a great deal of yelling to the players and umpires from the bleachers. In Fairfax County, winning is everything. But on the evening of the SOS's only exhibition game, everyone had fun. The audience was confused but entertained, the weather was perfect and the picnic dinner hampers held delicious food. The evening's play broke up when the twilight grew too dark to see well. In the end, everyone agreed they had a wonderful time.

"I was a pretty useless member of the team," Carol later confessed, "but it was more fun than I'd anticipated it would be."

Kym best summed up the experiences of the past four months: "Our cricket practices always began with a run around the park, and always ended with the ball in the poison ivy and Kurt falling in the mud."

Meanwhile, on the other side of the Atlantic Ocean, events had picked up speed in England. The BBC Oxford Radio station allowed Bill Drake to broadcast an appeal for a team of boys and girls to play cricket with a visiting group of American teens. Bill explained to Oxfordshire's listening audience that the Americans had just learned how to play the game, so experience wasn't necessary. He also mentioned that the Americans knew a lot more about the works of William Shakespeare than they did about cricket. He added that the Americans were looking forward to meeting boys and girls from England.

Bill got two responses. The first was from Mrs. Dobson who rang up, saying that she was the director of the Witney Swim Club and that some of her boys and girls were interested in playing a game with the Americans. Mrs. Dobson noted that the all the boys knew something about cricket, but none of the girls had ever played it, so it was probably a pretty even match up. Bill was absolutely delighted and accepted her offer immediately.

His second call was from Ms. Jane Walk, who was a program director from the BBC Oxford Radio. She was very interested in hearing about this unusual tour of American teens who were more fluent in Shakespeare than in cricket, and she wanted to have the kids do a late morning talk show interview on the day following the cricket match. Bill was ecstatic and said he would contact the Americans right away.

"Johnathon! Great news!"

"Do you know what time it is?" he growled. It was 6:30 a.m.

"I know, it's early, but I wanted to catch you before you went to work. Listen! I just got a phone call from Bill, the President of the Cricket Club in Oxford. He's the one who sent us the extra balls and now he's got us a team! A real team of teenagers. It's a swim club."

"Okay, so we're going to play this game in a swimming pool?"

At that hour of the morning, it was hard to tell if Johnathon was being serious or being funny.

"No, we're going to play at the Deddington Cricket Club Field. But that's not all."

"Does everybody have to wear swimsuits?"

"No, get serious. We are also going to be interviewed on the BBC radio on the day after the game."

"Interviewed?" He yawned loudly into the speaker. "Why?"

"I guess because the English have never heard of a bunch of American teenagers who act Shakespeare and who want to play cricket with a bunch of English teenagers who swim."

"I'm not sure that makes too much sense, but the interview will get our gang into a spin. You're talking about the British Broadcasting Company, right?"

"That's right."

"This trip is getting weirder by the minute."

Bill Drake followed up his phone call with a letter that outlined the particulars. The SOS would be playing opposite six boys and six girls from the Witney Swim Team at the Windmill Community Center cricket field on Sunday, July 10th – exactly two weeks away – at 4 p.m.

"I must confess, " he wrote, "that when John & Carol [Bessette] asked for two cricket balls, I didn't give it a second thought. But it seems to have stirred the unstirrable English too. . . We'll work the game accordingly. I rang Jane Walk a minute or two ago at Radio Oxford to thank her for setting it all up. Please contact her on your arrival at Oxford. All we need now is a classic English summer day."

Unbeknownst to us, Bill also sent a short publicity blurb to the Banbury GUARDIAN weekly newspaper. The following notice appeared in the July 4th issue:

"U.S. CRICKETEERS. An unusual match is to take place in the Windmill Centre at 4pm on Sunday when the Witney and District swimming club has a team of boys and girls who will challenge a mixed team of American high school students from Virginia.

"The Virginia team, who have been called 'the most unusual ball team in Northern Virginia,' have been training hard and are trying to get baseball out of their system. They wear black shirts, which will make it a change from our white. It should be an interesting match. Bill Drake will umpire, and he, and both teams look forward to the afternoon."

As the SOS had said when they voted to wear black shirts, "We're the outlaws!"

On July 2nd, the SOS had a Going-Away Party, hosted by Terri's parents. High spirits and loud noise went through the roof. For many of these kids, it was going to be their first time away from their parents and the first time away from home. For some, it was their first airplane trip and their first time traveling to a foreign country.

Everyone hated their passport pictures.

Each team member had remembered to bring an artificial flower to the gathering. Since the flowers were supposed to symbolize themselves, the collection was quite a mix. Besides the expected red roses, there were also violets, daisies, forget-me-nots, a blue iris, a tiger lily, a bird-of-paradise, and pussy willows all centered around a large, pink hibiscus. Steve's mom, who did flower arranging as a hobby, had volunteered to create a beautiful bouquet out of this eclectic flora. The SOS would leave this unique bouquet on Shakespeare's grave when they visited Holy Trinity Church in Stratford-on-Avon. To decide who would have the honor of placing the flowers, I drew names out of a hat. To represent the boys, it was Kurt, who was very pleased. The girls were represented by Molly. I prayed that Molly would not wear her red ballcap on the day we visited the famous gravesite.

The final bit of business, before the kids got down to the serious task of devouring pizza, was to sign baseballs. The SOS had decided to give each Witney team member an American baseball with all the SOS names autographed on it. For once, the kids repressed their urges to write oversize and they left enough room for the other twenty-three team members to sign. Passing the twelve balls around the room took some time, which was good because the pizza delivery was late.

Then it was time for the last minute check-list.

"Don't forget your passports. You can lose everything else you own, but not those passports. You have to guard them with your lives.

"Make sure you pack your team shirts – clean, a pair of white pants and yes, those blessed ballcaps. Remember, it's cooler in England, so you will want to wear long pants, instead of shorts.

"Don't forget your team duffle bags. Pack them with your overnight gear, toiletries and a spare set of clothes, just in case our suitcases get delayed at the other end. Please remember that the electric current is stronger over in England so you need a converter if you are taking anything that needs to be plugged in."

Hand in the air.

"Yes, Kurt?"

"Will we be taking our cricket gear?"

"No, we'll be using the bats and pads furnished by the Deddington Cricket Club. Finally, make sure each of you has some sort of wristwatch. You will be expected to be on time for everything for the next two weeks. Are we clear on that?"

Hand in the air.

"Are we having dinner on the plane?"

"I presume so. And I want all of you to try and get a good night's sleep on the plane – if possible. Once we land, we will be moving fast."

"Can I bring my teddy bear?"

"Absolutely. Does your Teddy have a passport?"

Fazil Karim helps Kym Samuels with the score sheets at the Exhibition Game.
(Paul Miller)

TEAM SOS AT DULLES INTERNATIONAL AIRPORT

Fairfax County, Virginia

JULY 5, 1988

Back row L to R: Jamie Fox, Paul Miller, Steven Fender, Keene Parker (team captain), Molly Pfaff, Kurt Bose and Zen Mason.

Middle row L to R: Kym Samuels, Nick Rose, Sabrina Sandusky, Katie Shirley, Libby Goodwin, Beckey Kelsey, Kathy Robinson, Terri Anderson, Meaghan Parker, Angela Kluwin, and Kaija Barlow.

Kneeling L to R: Ellen Caskie, Elizabeth Dettmar, Julie Zielaskiewicz (team co-captain), Susan Linsert (The Mighty Mite), Carol Blosser and Amy Pearson. (Johnathon Bigelow)

All present, even the Teddy Bear!

CHAPTER SEVEN
July 4 – 9, 1988

"Once more, dear friends, unto the breach."

Henry V

If there was a single word to describe the two-week SOS Tour of Great Britain, that word would be "rollicking". Also, "loud," "crazy," "unbelievable," "noisy," "hungry," "yelling," "confusion," "jokes," "eating," "screaming," "shopping," "running" and a whole lot of "laughter".

The Fourth of July was a night of packing and reorganizing for the Schallers. The next day was Lift-Off, or the Second Coming. Whichever way one looked at it, more Fairfax Shakespeareans were crossing the Atlantic. The SOS would leave for Great Britain on the morrow.

During the past five months, the team had worked HARD for this trip. The kids must have washed every car in Northern Virginia – twice! – and sold enough 'Shakesbears' to make a gingerbread bridge across the Atlantic. This group was more 'physical' than the first Shakespeare group of three years ago, and the SOS were definitely more active. The "look at me" attitude was rampant among them. I hoped that mind set would not get in the way of the trip. Since it was the year of the Summer Olympic Games in Seoul, South Korea, I felt as if I were taking Team USA to the Games, even though cricket is not considered an Olympic sport.

I was packed. My husband, Marty, was packed. Our dog was moping. The television was blaring and the refrigerator was bursting with enough food to last our daughter, Tori, for the next two weeks. Yesterday, the SOS had received their paychecks with all the money they had earned doing the fundraisers. During the past four months, Marty had acted as the banker for the money that the teens had earned as a group. He had kept track of who had washed cars, baked cookies, worked at the Folger Fun Fair and at their two huge yard sales. Using a complicated system of dividing the money by the number of hours each kid had worked at each event, Marty was able to figure out who got how much in their pay packets. Everyone seemed very surprised as well as happy with their earnings. They also got their luggage tags, their airplane seat assignments and probably more parental instructions than they could possibly remember. Suddenly, it was twenty-four hours to the check-in at the boarding gate.

A huge butterfly kept bumping against my ribcage.

July Fifth was a blur of activity, like whitewater rafting down a lively river. Breakfast and lunch were barely tasted. After looking at our check-off lists for the second time, Marty and I knew that we couldn't delay our leave-taking for another minute. Half the kids were already standing by the ticket counters at Dulles International Airport when we arrived. Everyone proudly carried their SOS duffle bags that now bulged with their worldly possessions. Anxious parents hovered on the fringes. The Bigelows arrived, looking excited and organized. The kids' noise level rose to the peak of the airport's high ceiling.

Call to order. A group passport check. Collected their medical permission slips with a silent prayer that we would never need to use one of these things. Ticket check. Then it was a round of group photos while the parents clicked away for "just one more picture." Team SOS created a low wall with their signature duffle bags and they posed behind them. Other people, hurrying through the airport, stopped to see who we were. Then lots of kisses and embraces.

"Good luck!"

"Be sure to mind Mrs. Schaller."

"Do you have your money?"

"Call us when you get there, so we know you're okay."

"Did you pack your vitamins?"

"Mom! Please!"

"Be sure to send a postcard to Mimi and Grandpa."

The kids looked relieved when we chaperons gathered the SOS together, counted noses, duffle bags , boarding cards and passports, then led the team through the gates to the shuttle bus that would take us to the boarding area. For once, the kids spoke to each other in subdued tones and sat close together in the waiting lounge. Trips to the restrooms. Trips to the candy and magazine stand. Trips to the water fountain. Finally, our flight was called. Another nose count, duffle bags count and boarding pass count, then we went down the boarding tunnel and onto the airplane. Twenty minutes later we shot down the runway for a perfect liftoff.

"It's really happening!" chirped Ellen in the seat directly in front of us. Her seatmates, Carol and Amy giggled.

Eight hours later and 3600 miles east of Virginia, it was now July the Sixth. Nobody had slept on the plane except the chaperons. When we landed at Heathrow Airport at 7 a.m. [British time], the skies were gray and moist, and it stayed that way until noon. Welcome to summertime in Merrie Olde England! At least a tour guide named Derek and a large, comfortable coach bus were waiting for us. As expected, there were some schedule modifications. The Trust Tour company had reworked my orig-inal wish list of places that I had sent to them back in November. Now it appeared that we would have even less free time than anticipated, and several sites had been changed.

Starting straight from the airport, there was a short stop at a motor-way convenience shop for "second breakfast" and snacks. The teens had a constant need for food. Then, while weaving in and out of the London morning rush hour, Derek gave a very good windscreen tour of Britain's capital city, including a stop in the middle of Westminster Bridge so we could take pictures of the Big Ben clock tower. It was windy and cool, but the kids, most of them still wearing shorts from ninety-degree temperatures in Virginia, seemed impervious to the weather. They took dozens of pictures of Big Ben. They took pictures of each other taking pictures of Big Ben. More than anything else, seeing that iconic clock tower proved to the SOS that they were really and truly in England.

Most of the kids thought we were standing on the real London Bridge, of "falling down" fame. There was no point in explaining that famous bridge was a few miles downriver. Team SOS were too excited and too jet-lagged to care.

After the bridge stop, our bus drove into the countryside of Kent on the way to Hever Castle. Kent was very lush with softly rolling landscape – truly "England's green and pleasant land." More picture-taking through the bus's wide windows. We finally arrived in the village of Hever and parked at the picturesque Henry VIII pub where the kids were served Ploughman's Lunches: fresh crusty bread, a wedge of sharp cheddar cheese, a pat of fresh butter and a helping of tangy Branston pickle. The food didn't appeal to most of the team. They looked at the Branston pickle as if it were a side dish of rat poison. Another thing about the SOS – they were very picky about what they put into their mouths. Ignoring the brownish pickle lumps, they whipped through the bread, butter and cheese quickly and were done eating before the chaperones had finished. Then the kids ran outside the pub to take more pictures.

Miraculously, the skies began to clear by the time we got to Hever Castle, once the home of Lady Anne Boleyn, the doomed second wife of King Henry VIII. Most of the group took this opportunity to explore a hedgerow maze. They loved the experience of getting lost in the midst of tall bushes. Afterwards, we toured the charming castle, which everyone enjoyed, especially Susan, who had put "visiting a real castle" at the top of her wish list. The gardens were next, filled with fanciful topiary, including a larger-than-life boxwood chess set. Lots more picture-taking. At this rate, the kids would run out of film before the end of the first week.

Mary W. Schaller

The next morning's dawn arrived too soon at our hotel in Greenwich which was downriver from central London. July Seventh turned into a rush-rush tourist killer. First was the visit to the infamous Tower of London – in the pouring rain. The kids loved meeting one of the Tower's famous Beefeater guards – more photos taken. Most of the SOS thought that the Crown jewels were overrated and they looked "'tacky". On the other hand, they were all fascinated by the ravens that were hopping freely around the grounds. The kids learned the legend that there must always be ravens living at the Tower or the British Empire would fall. On this particular day, the famous birds looked rain-soaked and miserable. The point of greatest interest was the graffiti carved into the stone walls of the room where the Dudley family had been imprisoned in 1554. The girls, especially, found Guilford Dudley's carving particularly sad. He was the nineteen-year-old husband of seventeen-year-old Lady Jane Grey. She was England's Queen for nine days, before Queen Mary Tudor took over the throne, and imprisoned the young couple for treason. They were executed on the same day, February 12, 1554. Guilford had carved the name "IANE" [Jane] on the wall of his cell. Our tender-hearted Elizabeth looked as if she might cry.

Lunch was at the historic George Inn in Southwark, across the Thames River from the Tower. It is a timber-framed pub that was built in the 1500s. Shakespeare's Falstaff would have felt right at home there. Very picturesque, quaint, and famous. Also very crowded with tourists. The kids didn't like this pub food here any better than they had at Hever. In the afternoon, we visited the London Dungeons, followed by the Southwark Cathedral, where Shakespeare supposedly worshiped.

The Dungeons were all grim and grisly, as they were meant to be. However, the live rats in the Plague exhibit were all fast asleep, which disappointed the boys. The Cathedral was truly beautiful, but we were only there for five minutes, before Derek rushed us back on the bus.

This whole day was done on a trot. The kids were not used to so much walking – nor hearing so much history in one long lecture. Derek presumed that we were unable to move anywhere without his help. Marty and I had decided not to tell him that we had lived in London for four years, because we didn't want to make him any more nervous than he already was. Derek felt that he had to keep us on the go every minute, or we wouldn't be getting our money's worth. Some of the team's parents had been worried about not keeping the kids busy. This was only the second day, and already, the SOS looked as if they were going to drop in their tracks unless we could slow the pace down. The five chaperones felt like we were on a Death March.

That evening, after a quick change of clothes and a wash up, we were driven back out into the countryside for a Medieval Feast at Hatfield House. Hatfield is a huge country manor house built in 1497 and was once the beloved childhood home of the great Queen Elizabeth I. The estate has belonged to the Earls of Salisbury ever since 1611. To make ends meet and to keep the roof from leaking, the current Earl of Salisbury hosted a nightly, roistering Medieval Banquet for paying guests, like us. The SOS had a fantastic time.

Dinner featured a delicious chicken with almonds dish, spiced pears and cakes for dessert, all of which the teens gobbled down. The Old Hall's "Medieval" entertainment was definitely a class act. The kids giggled at the mildly risqué songs and jokes. They participated in the singalongs, and they all joined the conga line at the end of the show. Even shy Paul got up and danced. Unbeknownst to the chaperones, Keene and Steve had gotten hold of some wine and mixed it with heady mead. The boys were about to experience the novelty of their first-ever hangovers.

Soft moaning was heard from the rear of the bus on our way back to the hotel following the Feast.

"Is somebody sick?"

"It's okay, Mrs. Schaller," Kathy said quickly. "You don't have to worry about it."

Not an encouraging message. Upon investigation, Steve and Keene look decidedly green around the gills.

"It's okay," Kathy repeated. "I'll take care of them."

"Food poisoning?" I hoped it wasn't going to affect the rest of us on the morrow.

"Not exactly," Kathy evaded. "Um, they just had too much to drink."

Warning bells. "Drink? Of what?"

"Um . . wine."

"How did a couple of underage teens get wine?"

Kathy sighed. "Remember when we all got up and danced around the Hall?

"Yes-s-s. And?"

"Well, Steve and Keene sort of drained all the wine glasses on the empty tables as they went around."

"Ye gods and little fishes!"

"And they also drank some mead with it." Meaghan added with a dark look at her writhing brother.

"How did they get the mead?" The Hatfield House version of this ancient libation was pretty heady stuff.

"Um . . . ah . . . "

Little Susan, sitting two seats away, answered. "I guess because I ordered some."

"You did what?" What were Johnathon and Marty doing at their end of the long table while the Mighty Mite was quaffing a liquor that was 100% alcohol?

"The menu said it was made from honey, but I didn't like it," she said in a small voice. "But Steve and Keene drank it and they liked it."

What were the waiters thinking?

"It's okay," Kathy reiterated. "Meaghan and I will take care of the boys. You can go back to your seat."

Since it was obvious that Steve and Keene were down for the count, I left them in the care of the girls and returned to the front of the bus. Brenda leaned over my seat.

"Tomorrow is the Free Day in London and those two are in my group. I'll make sure the boys will NEVER forget their tour around the city." She gave me a wicked smile.

If we had thought yesterday had been exhausting, July eighth should have been called "The Longest Day." Again, we were on the go from ten in the morning until midnight. This was the dreaded "Free Day in London," that so many parents had been worried about. They needn't have done so. The five chaperones ran their little darlings ragged.

As expected Steve and Keene wanted to stay in the hotel and sleep off their night of debauchery. They arrived at breakfast with red eyes, massive headaches and abject apologies.

"No, I'm sorry, boys, but the hotel doesn't want any of you hanging around during the daytime, and I can't leave you two without a chaperone, since we don't have any chaperones to spare." I gave each of them two Tylenol. "You're going with Brenda. She said she'd take good care of you."

And may the Good Lord have mercy upon your souls.

My group for the day were Nick, Angela, Kym, Amy and Kathy - a good workable bunch. Kathy, who had been up until two a.m. with Steve and Keene, was surprisingly wide-awake and in good spirits. She was the perfect travel companion. Always thoughtful, she would occasionally pause, and ask me if I were having a good time.

The kids had voted to see St. Paul's Cathedral, where Prince Charles and Lady Diana Spencer had been married in 1981. Kym and I visited the American Chapel where there is a large book inscribed with the names of all the Americans who had died in defense of England during World

War II. My father and Kym's great uncle are among the soldiers memorialized. Meanwhile, Nick and Kathy dragged poor Amy up hundreds of stairs to see the Gallery under the famous Dome. On the ground level, Angela enjoyed looking at the paintings on the walls in peace and quiet.

Afterward, we found a nice place to eat lunch near Covent Garden, and nobody complained about the food. Following lunch, the group had a short conference among themselves. We were supposed to visit the Theater Museum at Covent Garden, but Nick and the girls voted to skip the Museum and go straight to Kensington Gardens – the literary home of Peter Pan.

There the kids admired the life-size statue of Peter near the Serpentine and everyone took loads of pictures. They also had the chance to see – up close and personal – real swans with babies, a tern, mud hens, squirrels – and a live scurrying rat. The Kensington Palace gardens were in full summer bloom. More picture-taking.

We then caught a double-decker bus to Piccadilly Circus where we walked forever, trying to locate the Prince Edward Theater, where we would meet up with the others to see the musical CHESS. By now, poor Amy was practically sleepwalking, but she never complained. When everyone else finally arrived in front of the theater, I handed out the tickets, and the SOS dashed inside. The troops descended like locusts upon the CHESS gift shop and the snack bar, meanwhile "discussing" who was going to sit next to whom. After the requisite restroom visits, the chaperones finally herded everyone to the Upper Circle – nosebleed country – with five minutes to spare before curtain time.

This West End production of CHESS had its good points as well as bad points. The SOS liked the show, but everyone was disappointed by a very poor rendition of the show's hit song "One Night In Bangkok." The heavy-set gentleman, who sat on my left, was obviously bored as well. He snored.

Back at the hotel, I crashed into bed just after midnight and, for the first time on this trip, slept straight through till morning.

The following day, July ninth, we left the Ibis Hotel in Greenwich, and headed out of London on the first leg of our journey north. Derek was no longer with us, which was a relief. Our personable bus driver was Chris, a nice-looking young man, who was driving a tour bus as a summer job before he went to the United States in the fall to look for a permanent job there. His uncle owned the tour bus company, and he got Chris to agree to drive our group for two weeks by telling Chris that our tour was full of young American girls. His uncle "forgot" to mention to Chris just how young our girls were. When he first saw the thirteen-year-olds, Ellen, Carol, Amy and Susan, dragging their suitcases out of the Heathrow terminal, Chris realized that he had been duped. By then, it was too late. However, after his first full day with the SOS, Chris knew that he was going to have fun with us.

Our first stop was the town of Windsor, which was wall-to-wall tourists -- huge busloads of them. The kids wrinkled their noses and said that Windsor was too touristy and tacky. However, we did eat a good lunch at the Hart and Garter Inn – as in "mine host of the Garter" from Shakespeare's MERRY WIVES OF WINDSOR. This was a good choice of a pub, as the team had recently performed that play with Kurt playing the lead role of Falstaff. Lunch took up about half the time we were to spend in Windsor, but the meal was well worth it. And the kids were always happy with full stomachs.

The castle, itself, was a disappointment. After seeing Hever, the Tower and Hatfield House in quick succession, the SOS were becoming castle-jaded. The Chapel of St. George in Windsor, where the infamous King Henry VIII is buried, was closed because of a wedding. At least, we got to see some of the wedding guests in their finery, especially the men wearing top hats and tails, which Elizabeth especially liked.

Mary W. Schaller

Then we crossed a short bridge over to Eton, much to Zen's delight. The village of Eton was a lot less crowded and the High Street was very picturesque. Again, another disappointment. The College was also closed for a wedding! If we had booked a school tour, we could have gotten in, but good old Derek at Trust Tours had not done so, even though we had specifically asked for a visit to the College. Zen, understandably, was crushed.

Then it was back on the bus, and on our way to Oxford. Again, it was nice ride through the idyllic countryside. We arrived in the late afternoon. The SOS perked up the minute we crossed Folly Bridge and entered the famous university town. There were a lot of tourists in Oxford, as well, but at least, they were more spread out. Now that we were here, the SOS suddenly realized that the next day was THE DAY – our long-awaited cricket game. Excitement went up several notches.

First, we checked into St. Catherine's College where we would be spending the next two nights. St. Catz [the college's nickname] has very modern-looking buildings. Founded in 1962, it is Oxford's youngest college, but it has the largest undergraduate student body. The college is unique in that it was completely designed, inside and out, by the famous Danish architect, Arne Jacobsen. He created everything from the sleek, modern buildings to the built-in dorm furnishings, down to the STAR TREK- inspired knives, forks and teaspoons used in the Dining Hall. My room overlooked the grassy Quad. Since all the rooms were singles, Marty's room [yes, we were separated] was on the other side of the hallway, next to the Water Garden [or moat].

After everyone had dumped their suitcases in their rooms, the chaperones did the unthinkable – we turned the high schoolers loose on Oxford. Marlene, Paul's mom, took some of the younger kids for a stroll around the town. On the way to St. Catherine's, Nick had noticed a sign that advertised a performance of A MIDSUMMER NIGHT'S DREAM to take place that evening in one of the other colleges' gardens. He and Becky went off to have an early dinner before going to the play. Some of the other kids explored St. Catz's grounds. They quickly discovered the college's large cricket field behind the dorms, and they let off steam by running around the carefully manicured pitch, where they pretended to play cricket. Marty and I, together with the Bigelows, Zen, Carol and Ellen decided to go punting on the Cherwell River, which is a smaller branch of the Thames.

Punts are very long, heavy, flat-bottomed boats that one pushes along with a long pole. It looked easy enough. Johnathon, Brenda and Zen took one punt and they quickly disappeared up the river around the bend. Marty and I, with Carol and Ellen, had more difficulty with our boat. Marty poled and I paddled, and together, we managed to do a lot of initial circling in the basin, attempting to get the boat to go upstream instead of drifting backwards under the Magdalen Bridge. An audience of onlookers on the bridge shouted instructions and encouragement. Finally, we got the bow of our punt headed in the right direction. Then we zig-zagged our way upstream.

At one point, we accidently rammed a sleeping duck on a riverbank nest. The duck was not amused, although Carol and Ellen had fits of giggles. After about twenty more minutes of futile poling, we turned around and headed back downstream. Since the river's slow current made the return easier, Carol and Ellen took turns paddling the punt. We got back to the dock with little trouble where we waited for the Bigelows and Zen to come back.

Meanwhile, Carol and Ellen spied a nearby snack bar, and they asked if they could have ice cream.

"Ladies, I am not your mothers, and it doesn't matter to me, one way or the other, if you want to eat an ice cream before dinner. Go ahead."

The girls squealed with glee, hugged each other, ran to the snack bar and ordered large ice cream cones.

At this point, the other punt came into view with Zen paddling, Brenda poling and Johnathon sitting in the center of the boat like a pasha. Our Oxford adventure ended with shopping for college sweatshirts and an

Indian curry dinner, which the girls actually liked. We got back to St. Catz before dark, since the summertime sun didn't set until nearly ten o'clock. Brenda and Johnathon did a nose count at that hour, and were glad to find that all the kids, including Nick and Becky, were back on campus. Now everyone was room-hopping around the dorms. It appeared as if all the SOS had bought Oxford sweatshirts. Katie and Libby, who liked to wear identical outfits as often as possible, had purchased matching sweatshirts in a teal blue color.

While I was writing in my trip journal in my Danish ultra-modern bedroom, Johnathon appeared at my door with his notebook in hand.

"We need to pick the batting order for the game." He sat down at the student desk, flipped open his book and pulled out his pen. "We've got to do this now, so we don't have a long, drawn-out argument tomorrow on the bus."

The very thought of a "long, drawn-out argument" gave me chills. This was the first time that Johnathon and I had to actually choose our varsity team. Who were going to be our First Eleven? Deep breath. "Okay. So, who do you think should start? Keene? He's the captain."

"Yeah, but Jamie's the better batter. We've got to start off strong. Let's put Jamie first and put Keene as his partner."

"That sounds good. Who's up for third batter?"

"I'd say Kathy. She's one of our best hitters."

"And her partner in fourth position?"

"Kurt. He's also good, and he can't wait to bat."

Jotting down names in my diary. "Okay. And after him?"

"I'd say Terri. She's another good all-rounder."

"What's an all-rounder? We don't run any bases."

Johnathon chuckled. "It means that she's good at both wicket-keeping and at batting. And I think we'll put Steve up next as her batting partner. He can knock those balls out of the park."

Writing furiously. "Sound's good. Who's next?"

Johnathon took off his glasses and polished them on his shirttail – a sure sign that he was thinking deeply. "Well, that takes care of the boys. Paul takes pictures, and Nick hasn't been to any practices. So that leaves the rest of the girls. That's a lot of girls."

"Kym and Julie are scorekeepers," I reminded him.

"Yeah, but that still leaves a bunch." He studied his team roster. "Okay. Let's put Kaija up next. She can hit pretty good – and she's a fast runner. And Molly can hit; so we'll have her as Kaija's batting partner."

"Don't forget Zen. She'll kill you if she doesn't get to play."

"Right. She's up next, and we'll put Susan in after her."

Counting. "That's ten batsmen. Who will be the last one?"

Johnathon continued to polish his glasses for a few silent minutes. "Tough call. Amy, Katie and Elizabeth all want to play in the game. And they've earned it. They've come to every single practice." He put his glasses back on his nose. "Here's what we do. We put Amy as number eleven. The Laws say we can have a 'Twelfth man.'" He made quotation marks in the air with his fingers. "So that would be Katie."

"What about Elizabeth? She's the team's most ardent player."

"Exactly. The Laws also state that we can have any number of batters that we want to play, as long as that's okay with the other team and let's face it, we're not playing in a First Class Test Match here."

"Now, how about the bowlers?"

"Let's let Keene work that one out. We just have to make sure that all our bowlers get a chance to pitch. That includes the Mighty Mite. And both Terri and Kaija get to wicket-keep." He snapped shut his notebook, stood and yawned. "Looks like we've got our team. Everyone else can cheer. Are we done here?"

"Looks good."

"Yeah, now let's hope we have a nice day tomorrow. Cloudy would be even better." He went out the door and up the stairs to his room.

Meanwhile, there was quite a lot of noise and giggling going on at the base of the staircase on the ground floor. Looking over the railing, I saw Meaghan and Angela were standing inside a closet.

Meaghan, who had been collecting British magazines by the pound ever since we landed at Heathrow, had discovered the dorm's trash room. Zen, Carol and Ellen joined them and now all five of them were squeezed inside the Trash Room, dumpster diving through the huge, overflowing bins. Apparently, the college students had left lots of papers in their rooms when they had vacated the campus for the summer break a few days before we arrived. The SOS girls skimmed through the flotsam and jetsam, finding not only magazines and posters, but other interesting things like the Bodleian Library's rule book ["no pens, no fires"], St. Catz Fresher [freshman] welcome booklets, invitations to all sorts of parties during the past eight weeks, stickers advertising the college's production of "The Crucible" and someone's interesting study notes for the epic saga, "Beowulf". The trash of the dorm rooms was like an archeological dig of Oxford University student life, and the girls were having a wonderful time pawing through it. Intrigued, I scooped up a random handful of papers and went back to my room to look over them.

I was still reading though the Beowulf notes at 11 p.m. when I heard more muffled noise down the hall, coupled with a lot of "shh!," "shh!" Upon investigation, it was Kathy and the Mighty Mite sitting in front of a student-size refrigerator. It looked like they were trying to repair it.

"Girls! What's going on?"

Kathy looked up with huge wide eyes. "Nothing! Nothing to worry about. Sorry to disturb you."

Never a good sign. "What are you doing?"

"It's okay," said Susan.

"We're fine," Kathy added. She still had her hands inside the refrigerator. "You can go back to bed now, Mrs. Schaller."

Moving closer. "What are you trying to do?"

"It's okay. We're fine." Kathy didn't look fine; she looked stricken. Susan looked like a mouse caught in a large trap. "You can go back to bed."

By the looks of it, the fridge had not been defrosted in a year, and inside, frozen fast to the accumulated ice, were several fillets of sole.

"What is that? Fish?"

Dead silence. The girls looked at each other. Then Kathy gave a cough.

"Um, no . . . it's Steve's underwear."

"What?"

"Steve's underwear," the Mite repeated.

"Explain, please?"

Kathy stopped tugging the folded white chunks and wiped her hands on her pants' leg.

"Well, we thought it would be really funny to take Steve's clean underwear, and freeze it and then sneak it back into his suitcase."

How did they manage to get his underwear out of his suitcase? The girls must have done this in the afternoon while we were punting, because the clothing was now frozen solid.

Susan cleared her throat. "So, we came back here to get his pants, but now we can't get them loose." Kathy held up the dinner knife she had located in the nearby students' communal kitchen.

Time to make this a teaching moment. "Haven't you ever defrosted a refrigerator before?'

They shook their heads. They had probably grown up with frost-free freezers.

"First, turn off the fridge."

"We did that." Susan looked pleased that they had taken that precaution against self-electrocution.

"Good. Put the knife down. Now go into the kitchen and find some small bowls and fill them with the hottest water possible. And bring them out here."

For the next fifteen to twenty minutes, the girls ran back and forth from the kitchen with sopping bowls of hot water, which they slid into the fridge. While the water heated a small patch of frost, Kathy gently loosened the ice. Susan ran back to the kitchenette and dropped the icy bits into the sink. Finally, the girls managed to pry Steve's still rock-hard undies out of the fridge. They mopped up the damp pools on the floor, then turned the fridge back on and shut the door.

"Okay, ladies, now you figure out how and when you are going to return these to Steve. It would be nice if you defrosted them first. Hair-dryers work wonders."

Kathy and Susan didn't look too happy, but they were glad to see the last of the refrigerator. They scurried back to their rooms.

I wondered what would happen when Steve took his revenge.

On the other hand, that had to be the most creative prank to date.

The St. Catz clock tower chimed midnight. It was now July Tenth – and the day of our big Cricket Match!

DEDDINGTON CRICKET CLUB

The Windmill Center

Deddington, Oxfordshire

England

JULY 10, 1988

Bill Drake, President of the Deddington Cricket Club [left], greets members of the SOS Team and the Witney Team before their game. (Johnathon Bigelow)

Witney Swim Team member waits in the non-striker crease. Jamie Fox bowls while Kaija Barlow, in the Mid-Off position, watches. Bill Drake is the umpire in his white coat. The wind has picked up since the start of the game, as seen by the bending treetops and Bill's coat flapping. (Johnathon Bigelow)

CHAPTER EIGHT

July 10, 1988

"The game is afoot."

Henry IV Part 1

At 3:30 in the morning on July Tenth, I still hadn't slept since defrosting the refrigerator. Nerves – anticipation – worries kept nagging at my brain. What if it rained and we had to call off the game? There was no other day or time to play it; we had no wiggle room in our schedule. All those months the team had practiced in Rutherford Park's wretched field amid wax-melting heat, wet-blanket humidity, unrelenting poison ivy and acres upon acres of mud had to mean something. The SOS had to play their game today.

At 5:10 a.m., I was still awake. My insomnia was abetted by Arne Jacobsen's ultra-modern, rock-hard bed that made me feel like I was sleeping on a narrow shelf. Adrenalin raced through my system. Only ten more hours to go. In this dark and terrifying dawn, I wished we had never thought of playing a cricket match.

Prayed it wouldn't rain.

The team ate a quiet, sleepy breakfast in St. Catz's Dining Hall. We had been unable to have dinner there the night before because the Hall had been reserved for an alumni reunion, known in Oxford as a Gaudy. Breakfast was the usual fried eggs, Canadian bacon, toast and tea; the same menu that we had been eating for the past three days. By 8:30 a.m., Team SOS was wide awake, dressed, fed, and the kids were feeling antsy. They

Mary W. Schaller

were as anxious about the game as we adults were, although no one dared to say anything about nerves or the weather.

To kill some time before Sunday church services at eleven o'clock, we took a large group of the kids to the Oxford Story, a multi-media presentation of the Oxford student experience and history. The exhibition was a combination of light, sound, manikins and smells. It presented a really good history of Oxford. One exhibit showed a typical student's study/bedroom filled with papers and wine bottles. College students, who had seen this particular exhibit, said that this room wasn't messy enough. After combing through some of those papers the girls had scavenged from the trash bin last night, I understood exactly what these students had meant.

After the exhibition and browsing the gift shop, it was time to split up. The Bigelows took some of the kids to the Sunday service at Christ Church College Cathedral, where Charles Dodgson, aka Lewis Carroll, author of Alice In Wonderland, once worshipped. Marty and I took the Catholic group to Mass at St. Aloysius Church, where author C. S. Lewis, author of The Lion, The Witch and The Wardrobe used to pray.

When Mass ended an hour later, it had begun to rain. As our group trudged down the Woodstock Road, the rain grew heavier. None of us said a word as we splashed along looking for a place to eat lunch. The kids didn't dare ask if we were still going to play cricket today. After an unusually quiet meal at Brown's Restaurant, our group hurried back to St. Catz. It was still raining. Once inside the Porter's Lodge, I telephoned Bill Drake in Deddington and asked him if the game was still on. The SOS team clustered around the red phone booth in unusual dead silence. Their large eyes were full of hope, despite the ominous weather conditions.

Bill sounded jolly and optimistic. "Of course the game is on. The rain will stop."

I hung up the phone and opened the booth's door. "Believe it or not, it's a go! We're playing cricket today!"

Cheers from the kids. Outside the Lodge, the rain seemed to let up.

"Okay, everybody. Get dressed in your shirts and white pants. Better bring your jackets as it seems to be getting colder. And don't forget your ballcaps, please! We leave in a half an hour."

The SOS were dressed and on time at our bus. The rain had stopped. Chris sat behind the wheel wearing one of the kids' ballcaps and looking just as excited as the team. Now Chris was an official member of the SOS. He seemed delighted with his new hat. The trip was a thirty-minute drive up the A40 highway to Deddington. For once, the noise level was down as the kids talked quietly among themselves. They were about to meet real English teenagers and play the cricket game of their dreams. The tension and the energy inside the bus were palpable. On the way, Johnathon read out the batting order. No one objected; a few of the nonplayers even looked relieved.

The Witney Swim Team was made up of twelve boys and girls, approximately the same ages as the older members of the SOS. The English teenagers seemed nice, and they were just as curious about the SOS as the Americans were of them. Their adult leaders, Joan and Dot, were cheerful, welcoming and very enthusiastic, despite the ominous clouds overhead. The ladies had set up a number of board games inside the cricket club's modern observation pavilion at the Windmill Center. Large picture windows overlooked the field and it was blessedly warm and dry inside. The nonplaying members of the SOS made themselves at home, staking out claims of the chairs in front of the windows. Everyone held their collective breaths and hoped that the wet weather was over for the day.

Bill Drake was as excited as a kid at Christmastime, and he wasn't going to let a little thing like mud stop this cricket match. The SOS had traveled over 3600 miles to play this game. With a warm welcome to all, he gave introductions, pointed out the cricket equipment, including the pads that both teams would use, and showed everyone where the all-important restrooms were located. The Witney Team looked as nervous as the SOS did.

Then Bill led the way out to the pitch and both teams, including the non-playing members of the SOS, followed him to check out the field. Technically, the ground was a "sticky wicket," meaning that it was muddy in places, but Bill and Mr. Dobson, the other umpire, both agreed that the ground was still good enough for the game.

To the SOS, the Deddington Cricket field was a heart-stopping revelation. It appeared to be an ocean of the greenest, most well-manicured grass they had ever seen outside of a golfer's putting green. The grass looked like velvet. Up until this eye-opening moment, none of us, including the coach and manager, had ever played on a real cricket field. To our eyes, the oval looked huge. The one we saw in Washington could not compare to this one. Our pathetic little patch of ground at Rutherford Park was about a quarter of the size of this one at Deddington. The far boundary of the oval seemed to be a mile away.

"We're dead," Johnathon muttered. "We've been pulling in our batting for months so we wouldn't hit the cars, the woods, the baseball players or land in the creek. No one has practiced hitting a long drive." He pushed his glasses up the bridge of his nose, then called to our team captain. "Okay, Keene, time for the coin toss."

With an encouraging nod from Bill, the two team captains tossed a coin for first choice of position. The SOS lost the toss, and Witney elected to bat. Our 1st Eleven team plus Two huddled around Keene as he assigned the fielding positions. Kurt and Amy wore their team ballcaps. Molly wore her lucky red one. The rest of the SOS were bare-headed, despite the wet conditions. Keene elected himself to be the first bowler with Kurt as the second, and Terri was the first wicket keeper. Then the SOS ran out onto the field, cheering and clapping. The first two Witney batsmen stood at each wicket, staring at the exuberant Americans – and, at that point, the wind picked up and the clouds got darker

Most of the non-playing SOS members, as well as Brenda and Marlene Miller, retreated to the warm interior of the pavilion. Johnathon,

Marty and I stayed outside under a convenient overhang in order to be closer to the game, and to cheer on our chilled, but valiant team.

Despite the glowering weather, our scorekeeper Kym, wearing her tee shirt under a hoodie jacket, huddled on a chair nearby and enjoyed watching her teammates playing real cricket. "I was cold at the actual game – but that was fun too," she later wrote. "The British kids thought it was crazy that I had such a good understanding of how to keep score since they didn't. I thought that was pretty funny."

Because of the unstable weather conditions, Bill decided that the teams would play fifteen overs each, although he quickly amended it to twelve overs as the weather continued to worsen. Terri, wearing thick pads, took her place behind the wicket and watched the game unfold.

"We lost the coin toss to be at bat first. We didn't have a chance," she recalled.

Witney, going first, played all twelve of their overs, and made a total of 61 runs. Keene and Kurt alternated the first six overs. The boys later said it was hard to keep from slipping and sliding over the crease during the run up to pitch. The two extra players on the SOS side, Katie and Elizabeth, fielded while our other two bowlers, Jamie and Susan, were able to slip inside the pavilion to stay warm. That may not have been exactly legal, but at this point, it worked, and neither of the umpires noticed, nor objected. Jamie, the third bowler for the SOS, took down three wickets, which pleased him a great deal, and surprised both the other team and the umpires as well. The final two overs were bowled by the Mighty Mite, which may have been the biggest surprise of all for the Witney team as well as for Bill, who had not expected to see a female bowler, nor one so short.

"We couldn't get any outs," Terri later summed up the situation. "The boys on the English team hit a lot of balls well into the outfield. We never hit our balls that far – we weren't good enough. So, we didn't know how to field balls like that. As wicketkeeper, I had nothing to do but just watch in horror as the balls flew over our heads."

Team SOS fielding. [L to R] Kathy Robinson, Bill Drake [in the white coat], Terri Anderson, Elizabeth Dettmar, Jamie Fox [the bowler] and a Witney team member in the non-striker's crease. (Johnathon Bigelow)

By the end of Witney's twelve overs, the wind increased, and raindrops started to fall.

Bill wrote the following description of the game for the Banbury GUARDIAN:

"My left galosh filled quietly with water; the rain bucketed down in long grey sodden skeins, driven near-horizontal by a brisk, southerly wind. What, I wondered, standing at square leg, what the hell are you doing standing in a half gale in an umpire white coat, from which splashes dripped in big globules to the grass? But the [American] kids – that was the thing. To see those bright chattering youngsters run on to a wet meadow, all with logo T-shirts and some with logo baseball caps, was great. They ran, cheered, clapped, nattered, pitched [the greatest difficulty in bowling with a straight arm], batted, hit the stumps occasionally [more cheering], caught it seldom, slid whilst chasing, and by sheer exuberance, defied the elements."

When it was the SOS turn at bat, our boys were anxious to even up the score. Jamie, full of confidence, went first, taking his place on the striker's crease, while the wind increased its velocity. Keene, his batting partner, stood at the non-striker's crease and he prepared to dash down the pitch when Jamie hit the ball. Jamie swung at the first throw, hit the ball and . . . was immediately caught out, much to his disgust. Jamie was retired for the rest of the game.

Kathy, third in the batting order, took her place opposite Keene. She was not only the best batter among the girls, but she and Keene were also very good friends. They had known each other since 1984, when, as sixth graders, they had played the non-speaking roles of little cupids with brooms in TWO GENTLEMEN OF VERONA. Over the years, their friendship had deepened. On this trip, they were now considered a couple, although Keene and Kathy were quick to play down any romantic relationship. As long-time friends, they made an excellent batting partnership.

Kathy gave Keene a nod and a little smile of encouragement. Then he gripped the bat and waited for the first throw by Witney. The bowler whipped past Kathy and threw the ball. Keene hit it and he started running down the pitch toward the opposite wicket.

"Run, Kathy," Johnathon yelled, but she was already out of her crease and on her way. The two batters passed each other and were safe in their new positions before the Witney wicket keeper got the ball. First run for Team SOS! In the pavilion, the non-playing SOS members crowded the windows and applauded their teammates.

Now it was Kathy's turn at bat. The bowler ran and pitched. Kathy connected and sent the ball flying.

"Go, Keene," she yelled as she took off. They exchanged sides again while the Witney fielders tried to catch them out. The score now stood at two runs for the SOS; one each for Keene and Kathy.

The non-playing SOS members poured outside to the overhang to cheer on their team. Cricket is usually watched by a polite, sedate crowd, who applaud in between sips of Pimms Cups. Brenda had always imagined she would be at the cricket match, wearing a large wide hat and long skirt, saying "well played" and "good form." But today, it was, literally, a whole new ballgame.

The Witney team and the umpires were not expecting the American-style ballpark cheering that the SOS, led by Kurt, yelled across the field over the increasing rain.

"Hey, batter, batter, batter, batter, swing!" Kurt shouted as Keene again gripped the bat and stared hard at the Witney bowler.

Team captain Keene Parker, as bowler, waits to catch the ball as a Witney team member pops the batter's crease. The umpire is Mr. Dobson of the Deddington Cricket Club. (Johnathon Bigelow)

"Let 'er rip!" shouted Jamie.

"Come on, Keene! Show them what you got!" yelled Terri.

The other SOS girls just cheered!

The next pitch was once again wide. Keene shook the rain from his hair, then tapped the ground with his bat and waited.

On the next throw, Keene smashed the ball. Once again, Keene and Kathy exchanged sides. Three runs for the SOS!

"Do it, Cupids!" shouted Kaija, using the team's pet nickname for the two batsmen.

Kathy dug her feet into the muddy ooze of the crease and waited for the next pitch. It went wide.

At this point, the first over for the SOS was completed and the bowlers changed sides. Keene suddenly found himself facing a fresh bowler.

Watching SOS play in the rain and increasing wind, Johnathon whistled through his teeth. "The kids will be swimming between the wickets if this keeps up."

Heart pounding. "I can't believe how well they're doing."

"In this slop? Better than I expected. Okay, Keene's back at bat. He's ready."

"Hey, batter, batter, batter," Kurt yelled and clapped.

The Witney bowler threw the ball and Keene hit it hard once again. The ball flew over the fielders' heads. Both Keene and Kathy took off at dead runs, passing each other in the middle of the pitch.

Kathy skidded into the strike's crease. She wiped the rain from her face, then stared down the bowler.

The next pitch came hard and fast. Kathy slugged it and the two SOS batsmen again passed each other.

Now Keene was back to receive the next pitch. The ball bounced away to the right. Keene held his ground. At the other wicket, Kathy bounced lightly up and down. On the next throw, Keene slammed the ball and the two batters took off again, trying to maintain their footing on the slippery ground.

When Kathy reached the striker's crease, she looked up. The Witney wicket keeper still didn't have the ball.

"Run back, Kathy!" Johnathon shouted, just as Keene started back down the pitch again.

Kathy turned and ran, head down, back to the far wicket, passing Keene and literally skidding into the crease. When she looked up, she saw that Keene had also made it. Their SOS teammates on the sidelines went wild, jumping, cheering and clapping. Meanwhile, the trees around the edge of the field began to bend sideways in the wind.

"Double play!" Kurt shouted. "Do it again!"

Keene wiped the rain from his face and shook his sodden hair. He ran his hands down his wet pants, then prepared for the next pitch. When he swung, the umpire called "stumped out." Keene stared at him, not comprehending what had just happened. In his excitement, Keene had stepped outside of the batter's crease. The chalk line was there, but barely discernible in the mud.

His teammates clapped for him as he came off the field, but Keene was angry at himself. "Stupid, stupid," he kept muttering.

Meanwhile, Kathy still stood at the non-striker's wicket, and she looked after her partner with regret and understanding. Together, Keene and Kathy had scored a total of seven runs for the SOS.

Next up to bat was Kurt. Kurt lived and breathed baseball during the spring and summer months. He was the SOS's most devoted cricketeer. He had attended every practice at Rutherford Park. He worked hard on his bowling and fielding as well as his batting. He had chased the balls through mud, dust, poison ivy, briars, and often into the Long Branch stream. Now was his chance to make it all pay back.

"Come on, Kurt!" Kathy yelled down the pitch. "Get me home so I can hit!"

Kurt pulled his ballcap low over his eyes.

The bowler began his run, sliding a little as he came. He windmilled his arm back and pitched. Bouncing on the balls of his feet in anticipation, Kurt stepped forward, moved too far-- and crossed out of the batter's crease.

"Stumped out!" Bill called. Kurt all but threw down his bat in disgust with himself. His dream shattered. He knew that there were no second chances at bat, at least not in this game. He stalked off to the inside of the pavilion, not looking at any of his teammates who were clapping for him.

Kurt Bose at Deddington Cricket Club. (Paul Miller)

"Leave him alone for a while," Johnathon counseled. "He'll get over it, but it will kill him, if he thinks you feel sorry for him."

The fifth SOS batter up was Terri, having exchanged her keeper's padding for the striker's pads. She was confident that she would score for the team. Looking down the pitch at her partner, she saw Kathy shifting her weight back and forth.

"Let's go, Terri," Kathy called. "It's getting cold out here!"

But at this point, the second over was completed and the first Witney bowler was up again, putting Kathy back in the striker's position. "Oh, cripes," she muttered to herself. The bowler ran and pitched. The ball bounced in a puddle and splashed off-side. Kathy held her ground. The increasingly wet conditions and the stiff wind affected not only the batters' running abilities, but also the ball's action.

Kathy scrunched down and waited for the next throw. The ball bounced into a perfect position for her. She hit it hard and took off running. "Go, Terri!" she shouted.

For a split second, Terri looked a little startled, but then she tore out of her crease toward Kathy. They passed each other. At the batter's crease, the Witney wicket keeper still did not have the ball, so Terri spun in place and shouted "Again!"

Kathy tapped the popping crease at the far end, then turned. The two girls ran toward each other as fast as they could. One of the Witney fielders had overthrown the ball, sending the other team fielders off and running. On the sidelines, the SOS team jumped up and down and yelled all the louder. Kathy slid literally over the crease and nearly knocked against the wicket. She was safe, but muddy from hips to ankles. The score for the SOS now stood at nine hits.

The bowler caught the wayward ball, then backed up to make his run. Kathy gripped the bat's handle tighter. The throw was wide again, but Kathy held her ground and shook her head at Terri, who had stepped out of her crease. Terri scuttled back into safety. The bowler retrieved his ball, backed up again and bowled the next ball.

Kathy hit it and the two girls again changed places. Terri was getting impatient. She wanted to make a run. Now back in the striker's crease she lowered her head, rocked back and forth while she waited for the next throw. It came fast. The ball bounced further away than Terri had expected. She reached and hit it hard. Both girls started to run, when the umpire shouted, "Caught out!"

Kathy raced back to her crease. Terri looked around to see what happened. One of the Witney fielders had caught her ball. Dejected, Terri walked off the field.

"At least, I hit it," she said to Johnathon as she passed him.

"You did good!" he told her, but Terri silently disagreed.

Steve was the next batter up. He took his place in the striker's crease, thumped his bat on the squishy ground and look determined.

"Come on, Steve!" Kathy yelled down the pitch. "Let's go!" She ran her hand through the tangle of her dark, wet hair and squeezed out as much water as she could through her fingers.

The bowler hurtled toward the crease with his arm locked into position. With a wide, windmill throw, he pitched the ball at the tall, lanky American.

Steve connected, and he started his run down the pitch. Kathy was already out of her crease, when the umpire again shouted, "Caught out!"

Kathy again spun around and made it back to safety inside her line. Steve, realizing that his brief time at bat was now over, slumped off the field. Since that was the end of the third over, the Witney bowlers changed wickets. Kathy was once again the batter.

Kaija, batter number seven, scampered out to the non-striker's crease, with a huge grin on her face. She had been afraid that the game would be over before she had a chance to bat. Meanwhile, the wind had grown noticeably stronger. Now, the treetops seemed to flatten out in the gale. Just inside the pavilion's door, Molly started pulling on the soaking wet pads that Steve had discarded.

By this time, Kathy had been in play through four overs. She was now tired, wet to the skin and shivering, but the look in her eyes was still pure determination. She pulled in all of her considerable field hockey training as she waited for the next ball. The Witney bowler wiped the ball clean on his pants, then started his run. Kathy bounced a little in place to stay loose. As she swung her bat back, the umpire called, "wicket out!". Behind her, Kathy heard the wicket rattle. She had knocked off the bails just as Kurt had done.

After playing through four overs and making five runs, Kathy finally retired, slathered in Oxfordshire mud. She was angry at herself for doing something so stupid, but at the same time, she was happy to get indoors and have a chance to get warm and clean up a bit.

Molly was already on the field and ready to bat. The rain grew heavier. Both umpires scanned the skies.

The Witney bowler once again began his run, trying to keep his footing in the mud at the same time. He lobbed the ball down the pitch. Molly coolly waited then hit it for a long drive straight past the bowler and umpire.

"Let's go!" Kaija shouted, but Molly didn't need to be told what to do. She had been waiting for this very moment since the first day of practice back in March. The two girls ran nimbly across the pitch, exchanging sides. One more run for the SOS! The SOS cheering section retreated back against the wall of the pavilion in a futile effort to get out of the wind.

Kaija finally had her turn at bat. When the next ball came, she hit it hard and started running. Molly sprinted out of her crease and the two girls high-fived each other as they passed. Another run!

The wind increased. The rain seemed to be pelting sideways. The bowler backed up for his next pitch to Molly. At that moment, the rain turned into hail and the wind howled louder. The umpires looked at each other, then Bill announced that the game was over. Without an argument, both teams gratefully fled for the pavilion.

"We were so relieved when it started raining and the very, very lop-sided game was called off," Terri confessed later. "Then we could all go inside and talk, which we kids most wanted to do."

Kym, who had stuck it out to the end as the scorekeeper, was the last member of the SOS to leave the field. Her papers were wet and scribbled.

"I just need to get some dry paper and I'll give you the score sheet," she promised.

"What was the score?"

"Witney 61; SOS 11."

"So we lost."

Not exactly.

While the teams rushed to the restrooms to use the hand driers and wring out their clothes, Bill and Mr. Dobson met with Johnathon and me. Despite the fact both men were soaking wet, they were all smiles.

"Brilliant!" Bill complimented the SOS team. "Your boys and girls did a jolly good job! Your batter, the one who made the five runs, she stayed in a long time – for a girl."

I thanked Bill for his compliments, but decided not to tell Kathy the part about playing well "for a girl." Being an ardent women's libber, she would have been offended.

"I wish it hadn't been such bad weather. Maybe, we could have done better. But the kids didn't expect to win anyway," I said.

Bill grinned and raised one silver eyebrow. "Win?" he echoed. "Nobody won. The game was a draw."

Johnathon cocked his head. "How's that? Witney had a score of sixty-one."

Bill shook his head with a smile. "Ah, you Yanks! Bless you. That's not how we play cricket here. If the game is declared a draw – and many Sunday afternoon games end that way – then no one wins and no one loses. The scores do not matter."

"Interesting," said Johnathon.

Heart in my mouth. "Does that mean the SOS can say that we are still the undefeated cricket champions of Fairfax County, Virginia?"

"Exactly."

"That will cheer up the team."

The SOS were extremely fortunate to have had the Witney Swim team as their opponents. Despite the fact that none of the English girls had ever played the game, and that the match was held in a chilly, windy downpour, the Witneys showed remarkable good sportsmanship, as well as good humor, throughout that stormy afternoon. Team SOS was forever grateful to the Witneys for making their cricket dream come true.

The Witney kids and their moms had brought a delicious spread of food. The SOS contributed Snickers Bars and Tootsie Rolls – all-American candy. [Jamie had brought the Snickers.] The SOS also passed out the autographed baseballs to the Witney players, who looked a little surprised by this unusual gift. Then, from the depths of the SOS duffel bags, a number of the elusive SOS ballcaps appeared. Zen, Kathy, Kym and some of the others wrote their names and addresses inside the hats and then gave them to members of the Whiney team, who appeared delighted to have the much-reviled caps. Kurt kept his hat firmly on his head. Then all the teens, both American and British, attacked the waiting platters of sandwiches, scones and jam, cookies and delicious slabs of sponge cake.

One of the Witney boys, Steven McCormack who went by the name of Mack, told Terri that this was the first time he had ever eaten a Snickers Bar. The Brits had their own version called a Marathon Bar, but Mack and the rest of the Witneys liked the Snickers better. That American candy bar made a huge impression on the English kids and went a long way to cement international relations between the teams.

Several games of Trivial Pursuit started in between mouthfuls. Unexpected by all of us, Ellen, the second youngest SOS member, proved to be a Trivial star.

Hot sweetened tea in deep mugs was especially welcome among the soaking wet adults. The excited hum and buzz inside the Deddington Cricket Club pavilion indicated that the American kids had achieved their goal. Having mutually survived the wind and rain in a game of cricket, the social ice was already broken and there was very little shyness among the teenagers. The six Witney boys found the eighteen American girls to be fascinating, while the SOS boys charmed the six Witney girls. Addresses were swapped. Everyone promised to write.

Terri and Mack's friendship has lasted decades. Over the next few years after that epic game, Mack visited the U.S.A. and Terri on several occasions. He was sometimes accompanied by his Witney teammate, Mark Thomas.

The porter at St. Catz had made it very clear to us that the team must be back at the college for dinner at 7, so at 6:30, the chaperones dragged our kids away from their new-found friends and the remaining delicious food. As Chris drove slowly out of the Deddington Cricket Club grounds, the SOS hung out the bus windows waving to the Witneys. All the way back to St. Catz, the kids laughed and chatted about their new-found friends. The SOS's dream of meeting real English teenagers that the team had back in February had been fulfilled in more ways than they had ever hoped. It made every hot, humid day playing cricket at Rutherford Park worth the blood, sweat and the occasional tears.

We arrived back at the college, wet and cold, in the nick of time to get – cold meats, liver pate and crackers, with slim pieces of cake for dessert. It was a typical Sunday supper at St. Catz.

"We should have stayed at Deddington," Brenda grumbled. After dinner there was a general rush for the college's showers and washing machines. The chaperons repaired to the college's student pub for stronger liquid refreshment.

Weeks later, after we returned to the United States, I received Bill Drake's description of the cricket game that he had written on June 11th for the Banbury GUARDIAN:

"In the end, in a mud pile, we called it a day. The score was immaterial and I doubt it was accurately recorded, anyway. I tried to explain a 'by' to the wicket keeper [Terri], a lovely young lass drowned in pads and large, blue keeper gloves. Mrs. Dobson and the Witney team provided a lovely tea and Trivial Pursuit kept them busy for a bit. But they [Team SOS] made contact with the natives, perhaps for the first time escaping from the grinding tourist capsule. That was the intent and we succeeded. Perhaps a few addresses were swapped and friends made. Today [July 11th] Mary goes on Oxford Radio and the bus 'does' Stratford. Mecca. Then Scotland – London and home. Good, dear old Yanks! Find me a quiet, leafy Virginian backwater university, and I'll study you more closely. God knows what Scotland will be like if this weather persists!"

Miraculously, no one caught cold. The following day dawned bright, dry and brilliantly sunny.

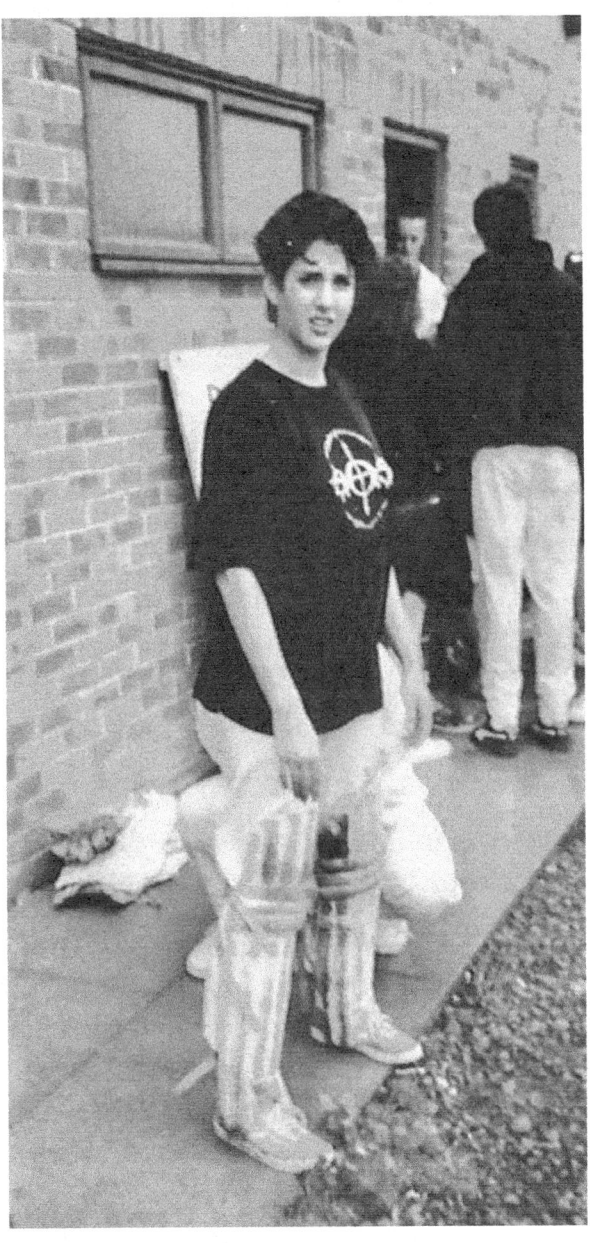

Kathy Robinson, exhausted and drenched, waits while a teammate unbuckles her padding. (Mary Schaller)

HOME CLUB	Witney Swim Team	V Shakespeareans	AWAY CLUB	PLAYED AT Daddington Cricket Club	DATE 7/10/88	WEATHER CONDITIONS Raining, windy		RATE PER OVER

SOS batting table (handwritten scoresheet):

	BATSMAN	TIME IN/OUT		HOW OUT	BOWLER	TOTAL
1	Jamie Fox	//		Caught		0
2	Keene Parker	1 · 1 · 2 //		Stumped		4
3	Kathy Robinson	1 · 1 · 2 · 1 //		Wicket		5
4	Kurt Bose	//		Wicket		0
5	Terri Anderson	//		Caught		0
6	Steven Fender	//		Caught		0
7	Kaija Barlow	1 ·		Not Out		1
8	Molly Pfaff	1 ·		Not Out		1
9	Suzen Mason					
10	Susan Linsett					
11	Amy Pearson					

TOTAL	11	FOR	2	IN	4

UMPIRES: Bill Drake + Mr. Dobson
RESULT: Draw - Called on account of rain

Bowling analysis:

	BOWLER	WIDES	NO BALLS	OVERS	MDNS	RUNS	WKTS
1	Keene Parker			3		0	
2	Kurt Bose			3		0	
3	Jamie Fox			4		3	
4	Susan Linsett			2		0	

PRINTED IN GREAT BRITAIN

COPYRIGHT THOMAS SCOREBOOKS 1984

THE SOS SCORESHEET
SOS vs Witney

This record, kept by Kym Samuels, indicates the SOS batting order, the number of runs each batter made and how they were out. Kaija and Molly were on the field when the game was called so they are designated as "not out." Zen, Susan, Amy, Katie and Elizabeth never got the chance to bat because of the weather. The score sheet also indicates the SOS's bowling record. Keene bowled first when the ground was reasonably dry. His three overs equaled 18 throws. Kurt was next also with three overs or 18 throws. Neither boy knocked over a Witney wicket. Jamie, the third bowler, completed four overs for a total of 24 throws. At this point the ground was wet and slippery, which is why he took one of Susan's overs. He knocked down three wickets which was a stunning achievement. Susan, the Mighty Mite, bowled the last two overs or twelve throws for the inning. She experienced the wettest ground but managed to keep her footing.

CHAPTER NINE

July 11 - 17, 1988

"Stands Scotland Where It Did?"

Macbeth

The next morning, July Eleventh, everyone slept late. After another egg and Canadian bacon breakfast in St. Catz's Hall, the SOS boarded their bus, and by 10:30 a.m. we were on the way to our next stop – the BBC Radio Oxford studio. Most of the team wore their new Oxford sweatshirts. Now that the anticipation and the stress of the cricket game was over, the SOS relaxed and were noisier, if that were possible. Chris located the studio building in north Oxford. Johnathon and I took Elizabeth, Keene, Kurt, Kathy, Julie and Zen inside while the others waited in the bus. Chris tuned in to the radio station so that everyone on the bus could hear the show.

The BBC people at the studio were very nice. As it turned out, only three members of the team could fit inside the narrow broadcast booth at the same time, so Johnathon [cricket Coach], Keene [team Captain], and Elizabeth [the team's Spokesperson] took their places next to the interviewer during a commercial break. The rest of us watched from the control room.

Jane Walk of the BBC very kindly recorded a copy of the interview which had very little to do with cricket, and a lot more to do with the Shakespeare class. Keene surprised and amazed his teammates by answering the interviewer's questions in a mature and thoughtful manner. Elizabeth was the team's perfect representative and she clearly enjoyed the whole experience. After getting our taped copy of the interview and BBC Oxford Radio stickers for everyone, we left the studio and fled for the bus.

On the way up to Stratford-on-Avon, Chris replayed the interview tape on the bus's sound system. Elizabeth turned beet red when she heard her voice on the radio.

"Ooooh! I can't believe I said that!"

"Don't worry; it was great!"

"Does my voice really sound like that?" Elizabeth asked everyone. Everyone assured her that she sounded fine.

"Keene, you did a good job," Zen complimented him. "I didn't know you could talk in polysyllabic words."

Keene just shrugged his shoulders and slid further down in his seat.

Upon arriving in Stratford, the first stop was Anne Hathaway's Cottage for lunch as well as a Photo Opportunity. A lot of the group chose to tour the famous home where a young Will Shakespeare had wooed the much-older Anne. Susan asked to have her picture taken in front of the cottage, just as her mother and great-aunt had done in years gone by. Susan was happy to keep up her family's tradition.

Lunch in the Rose Garden Cafe was delicious, but the SOS quickly discovered they were not the only ones interested in their food. Six ducks watched the entrance to the picnic tables very intently as we came out with our food trays. The six ducks rapidly expanded to twenty-three. Everyone was surrounded by ducks. They seemed to have no fear of humans and were begging at the tables just as a dog would do. Swallowing their last crumbs, the SOS fled for the safety of the bus. Sometimes meeting the locals could be a little scary.

The next stop was the second most important one of the whole trip -- Holy Trinity Church in Stratford-on-Avon, where William Shakespeare is buried. Some members of the SOS had been in the Shakespeare classes for over five years. All of them had acted in three or more of his plays. Now, they were going to be standing within a few feet of the earthly remains of the actual man.

"I've got goosebumps," whispered Sabrina.

First, the group posed outside the church for a special photo before going into the holy of holies. It was like herding cats to arrange the kids to stand in a pleasing formation around Kurt and Molly, who held the bouquet.

"Don't push!"

"You're stepping on my hand. Get off!"

"Don't block me. I want to be in the picture, not just be a part of your head!"

"Are we done yet?'

"Just one more shot, kids! This is for your memory books."

"I don't have a memory book!"

"Trust me, you will. Hold still, everyone, and smile! You are here! In Stratford! And you will be visiting Mr. Shakespeare himself."

"I hope we don't see his ghost"

"Ewue!"

Despite the snipping, once they were inside Holy Trinity, the atmosphere of that venerable church enveloped the group. There was not a sound out of any of them. The flower-laying itself was a short, simple but moving ceremony. Everyone gathered at the velvet rope in front of the altar. Then Molly and Kurt were escorted by the church verger beyond the ropes to the actual gravesite on the paved floor to the left of the alter. In silence, they knelt down together and placed their esoteric flower arrangement on the grave stone itself. They carefully arranged the bouquet's pink, green and gold ribbons that had been used in our production of OTHELLO. They opened the card that everyone had signed and left it standing beside the flowers. Then Kurt and Molly withdrew quietly. No one spoke a word until we were outside again. Speaking in awed tones, the kids said how much they had liked that visit, and how special it had been to see their flowers placed on Shakespeare's grave.

Our rooms at the famous White Swan Inn in Stratford were scattered over several different floors. The hotel, created from several 16th century buildings, was a maze of corridors, turns, lots of stairs and no elevators. By this point in the trip, most of the kids were beginning to hate their suitcases. At the rate they were buying souvenirs, their bags must have been getting heavier daily.

It was now 4 p.m. and we had to be dressed for the theater and ready for dinner by six. We decided to give the kids the option of visiting the Shakespeare Birthplace or doing some shopping and sight-seeing on their own. The group were very happy with that arrangement. They had been constrained inside the bus for most of the day. About ten of them went to visit Shakespeare's Birthplace. Several others went rowing on the Avon River, and the rest went shopping. Everyone made it back to our hotel on time, clutching more bulging shopping bags. After a quick dinner, Chris drove the SOS over to Stratford's Royal Shakespeare Theater, which was packed. We got to our seats just before the curtain rose. The team looked wonderful: clean, brushed and dressed in their good clothes.

The play was THE TEMPEST, one that all the group knew well as many of them had acted in the class production of it. The big surprise was that the part of Prospero was played by John Wood, whom the kids had seen in such movies as "War Games," "Lady Hawke," and "Lady Jane." The even bigger surprise was that he was performing with a broken leg, injured during the past week. This night he was acting without the use of crutches or pain killers, and by the end of the three-hour performance, he was obviously in pain. Nevertheless, he did a terrific job. The kids enjoyed the play immensely. Mr. Wood's performance was awe-inspiring and an excellent example of the famous adage: "The show must go on."

After the play, we went back to the hotel, and the chaperons went to bed. A lot of the kids stayed up all night, talking to each other or to the hotel's night porter. This wasn't a big surprise. By now, most of the kids stayed up every night, and everyone slept on the bus during the day.

July the Twelfth found our intrepid cricket team heading north toward the lowlands of Scotland by way of Warwick Castle. This rambling fortress, begun in 1066 by William the Conqueror, was a great hit with everyone. The Castle was a huge, romantic pile of stone with turrets, winding staircases, a portcullis over the entryway and a replica of the grim Rack in the dungeon. The hit of our Warwick visit were the seven resident male peacocks who were in full fantail display in a futile pursuit of one disinterested peahen. The kids scooped up fallen feathers from the ground, and they stalked after these fearsome birds in hopes of more loose feathers. Lunch, always the favorite activity of the SOS, was in the castle's café. Afterwards, it was back on the bus, count noses, do a passport check and we were finally off to Scotland.

Since our driver, Chris, was required by law, to take a half hour break every four hours, we pulled off onto a tiny byway near Carlisle and next to Hadrian's Wall, the ancient Roman-built boundary between England and Scotland. Chris located a nice turnout next to the ruins of a crumbling Roman watchtower, where he could park the bus and relax.

The history of this ancient wall and the antiquity of the stones were only minor attractions, as far as the kids were concerned. The SOS scrambled out of the bus and into the glorious afternoon sunshine. They leapt over the low-lying Roman stones to play frisbee in the gently rolling pasture beyond. The English landscape was straight out of the PBS show "All Creatures Great and Small." For the SOS, the field presented a great opportunity to let off steam.

One thing that was not covered in our Cultural Sunday briefings was the existence and nature of something that none of these suburban kids had ever seen – cow paddies. They couldn't believe how big they were, nor how smelly. Some of the kids actually took pictures of an especially large specimen.

Meanwhile, several of the girls discovered something else equally foreign that was growing on the roadside, beautiful, purple, prickly thistles – the official flowers of Scotland. They gingerly managed to cut several blooms without getting too many prickles from the bushes and leaves. Chris helped them fabricate several "vases" out of empty plastic soda bottles. Then, it was everyone back on the bus, but at least the kids had been able to run around thistle bushes, and jump over cow paddies – two things they had never encountered in Rutherford Park.

Soon we drew near to the actual line between England and Scotland. Chris made the announcement over the bus's PA system that everyone needed to get out their passports because we were coming up to the Scottish border. The kids believed him, and they quickly pulled out their little booklets, then looked expectantly out the windows for the official barrier and gatehouse. The adults tried not to laugh out loud at the joke.

Just as we crossed the line, it began to rain once again. Welcome to Scotland!

While the SOS had found England to be too touristy, tacky and crowded for their tastes, they embraced Scotland to their hearts. They loved the wild, misty beauty of the countryside and the fact that the roads were practically empty of tourist buses most of the time. Perhaps they related more to Scotland than to England because thirteen of them had performed in the class production of MACBETH in 1987. Zen had been a chilling Lady Macbeth, while Nick played the Drunken Porter. Julie, Kaija and Sabrina had great fun as the Three Witches who conjured a ghostly Becky, one of the prophetic spirits. Kathy brought a certain pathos to her role as Lady MacDuff, and Paul made a regal King Duncan. One of Kym's favorite roles was Fleance and Kurt was believable as the bloodstained First Murderer. Katie and Libby, who played the Scottish noblemen, Ross and Angus, had to be persuaded not to dress in identical plaid kilt skirts and scarves. All the kids knew the story of the doomed Thane of Cawdor and Glamis.

The Most Improbable International Cricket Team Ever: A True Story

Now that the team was actually in Scotland, the grey, damp scenery stirred their imaginations of a land filled with magic and myths. The teens soon discovered that Scotland also had the best shopping of the trip.

Our first overnight stop was in the quaint little town of Moffat, known for its woolen products. In fact, the central feature of the town square fountain was a statue of a large sheep. The Moffat Weavers Outlet was practically on our hotel's doorstep. The eighteen SOS girls, who were experts in the fine art of shopping, did a lot of window-gazing and begged to have more time here on the following morning so that they could do some serious spending. Following a brief consultation with Chris, the chaperons agreed. After dinner, the adults went to bed early, while the kids stayed up most of the night, as usual.

The next morning after breakfast, our gang were standing at the Outlet's doors when they opened at 9:30 a.m. Like starving locusts, the SOS descended upon the plaid and wooly merchandise, and they embarked on a shopping frenzy. Cable knit sweaters, plaid kilts, scarves, tams, gloves, socks as well as Scottish dolls, figurines, black Scottie toy dogs disappeared off the shelves with alarming speed. It seemed as if the kids had bought everything in sight, mostly as gifts for their families.

After loading up the bus with enough woolen purchases that probably equaled a flock of sheep, we headed up the highway to Glamis Castle, the childhood home of Britain's revered Queen Mother [1900-2002]. Perhaps because Glamis was the sixth castle that we had visited on our tour so far, the SOS were growing tired of the turrets, large paintings and gilded furnishings. The castle looked more like a French chateau than a romantic Scottish fortress, and the guided tour was only mildly intresting, perhaps because the current family who lived there, the Earls of Strathmore, did not emphasize the Macbeth connection very much, even though Glamis was the scene of the murder of King Malcom II in 1034, a true incident which may have inspired Shakespeare's play.

The young Shakespeareans Over Seas much preferred eating lunch in the the castle's café. Then everyone clambered back on the bus and we were off through gorgeous forested scenery.

Our next overnight stop was the biggest surprise of the trip. Set high on a hill, overlooking stunning countryside, was a sumptuous Victorian health spa. Built in 1878, it was now the Stakis Dunblane Hydro Hotel. Constructed in the era of Grand Spa Hotels, it featured a posh, velvet-lined lobby, uniformed bellboys, tennis courts, an indoor pool, a whirlpool, several bars and a night club. The kids were thrilled. The chaperons were agog.

"Chris, are you sure we are in the right place? This hotel looks pretty fancy for us."

He grinned and pointed to his directions. "That's what is says here."

"Wow!"

"Mrs. Schaller, is this where we're staying?"

"Can we get off the bus now?"

Deep breath. "Okay, people, it seems that someone in our tour agency lost their minds and booked us into this ritzy establishment. You WILL be on your best behavior here. No running up and down the halls. No yelling -- anywhere. Remember there are other people staying here besides us. And, at all times, remember you are representing the United States of America!"

"Can we get out now?"

The kids dressed in their best clothes for dinner, which tasted delicious, and the service was impeccable. No one complained. The adults had wine. Ellen refrained from balancing one of the silver teaspoons on her nose – a trick she often did to amuse us at mealtimes.

After dinner, we went into the disco to see some Scottish dancing, as advertised on the placard at the entrance. This was better than any of us had expected. The warm-up dance band was great and all of us got out on the floor -- and waltzed. Then we learned a circle dance called the Bird that involved a lot of flapping elbows. This was followed by a square dance-type of reel that reminded us of the Virginia Reel and most of the kids picked up the steps quickly. One thing about traveling with twenty-four extroverts – not one of them was shy about performing. When the band leader asked us where we came from, the kids shouted "Virginia!," so for the rest of the evening we were called the Virginians, as if we were a rare and exotic tribe. Following the dancing, the star attraction was introduced.

He was the reigning National Champion Highland Dancer, and he was incredible. The kids were captivated. Here they were in Scotland, watching a real Scotsman dance to the music of real bagpipes. After an unforgettable exhibition of Highland dancing and bagpipe playing, the Champion came over to where the SOS was sitting, and he asked the Mighty Mite to dance with him. Susan didn't miss a beat. With a huge smile, she took his outstretched hand and joined him. She looked adorable dancing in her new Moffat plaid skirt with this tall, dashing Scotsman in swirling kilts. After that, everyone was invited to get up and dance. The floor was filled with people of all ages from Great Britain, Germany and America – everyone leaping, laughing and twirling to the music. Even our driver, Chris, joined in. Carol and Ellen partnered a couple of Scottish boys, and together the four of them danced away the rest of the evening. Exhausted, we finally got everyone to bed around midnight.

Becky and Nick had reserved one of the tennis courts for an early morning match. Later, rumor had it that Becky had beaten him soundly, although neither Becky nor Nick ever mentioned the game. Nick should have remembered that she was a member of her school's varsity tennis team.

The breakfast buffet was the best one we had eaten on the trip, not just eggs and Canadian bacon. Then it was everyone back on the bus. At that moment, the rain began to pour down.

Hand in the air. "Can we stay here one more night?"

"I wish, but we're supposed to be taking a boat trip on Loch Ness."

Everyone looked out at the rain that now pelted against the bus's windows.

"Do we have to take a boat ride?"

"It's raining."

"And it's cold."

Agreed, three hours on a windy and rainy loch certainly didn't sound like much fun. Chris and I went into a huddle.

"Do you want to skip the boat ride? They probably are canceling it anyway because of the weather," Chris pointed out.

"We could, but what will we do with the kids? Take them to Cawdor Castle today?"

"Let's stay here!" Zen suggested again.

Chris thought a moment. "Well, Blair Castle is nearby. We could go there today and do Cawdor tomorrow, like you planned."

"But can we get into Blair? We don't have a reservation."

Chris just smiled. "I can fix it, boss lady."

"Okay, let's do it." Castle number seven, or was it eight? "Listen up, folks, we are going to Blair Castle today. It's inside; it's warm. And it probably has a gift shop."

No grumbling. In fact, most of the team slouched down in their seats for a mid-morning snooze. Chris's suggestion turned out to be a good switch. The minute the bus left the highway and drove down the long, tree-lined avenue to Blair, the kids perked up. When castle came into view, they were sold on it.

"Ohh! It looks like Cinderella's Castle in DisneyWorld," said Susan.

Like Disney's dream castle, Blair was white and had a lot of turrets. Just as we pulled up to the parking lot, the rain stopped, and a piper appeared outside the front door, wearing full dress kilts and playing his bagpipes. Blair is the home of the Duke of Athole, and it has been in the same family for over four hundred years, which gave the owners a lot of time to cram it full of stuff. The main hall literally bristled with lots of sharp, pointy weapons like Claymore swords, long-handled pikes and muskets with bayonets. In addition, the walls were full of deer antlers, like the ones we had seen at Glamis. The Scots were obviously very fond of displaying all their hunting trophies.

After an hour's guided tour of gilded furniture, and long halls hung with large paintings, we ate lunch in the castle's café, which satisfied all our picky eaters. Then the kids loaded up on candy bars and more plaid items at the gift shop.

Back on the bus, we headed onward and upward into the mountains. The beautiful scenery impressed even the most jaded members of the group. White, wooly sheep grazed on the hillsides that were vivid with green foliage. The sun played hide-and-seek with the cloud-capped mountaintops. In a word, the Highland scenery was awesome.

On a whim, Chris stopped the bus about ten miles outside of Inverness to visit the Culloden Battlefield. This wind-swept moor was the place where the Scottish clans were nearly wiped out by the English army, led by the Duke of Cumberland, in April 1746. Following his defeat in the battle, Bonnie Prince Charlie Stewart, the Pretender who wanted to reclaim the English throne from Hanoverian King George II, fled for his life to the Isle of Skye. Culloden, scene of the last pitched battle in Britain, is as important to the history of Scotland as the Battle of Gettysburg is to Americans.

It was nearly five o'clock in the afternoon when we got out of the bus at the battlefield on Drummossie Moor. The skies were pewter grey and the wind whipped around us.

A teaching moment here. "Think of Macbeth. This is just the type of place where he would have met the three witches."

"When shall we meet again, in thunder, lighting and in rain?" Kaija intoned one of the witches' speeches. She looked across the barren, rock-strewn battlefield.

"That will be ere the set of sun," replied several teammates.

"Just like now," Zen added, in a hushed voice.

On that barren moor, one could almost see the witches cackling around their steaming cauldron. This battlefield evoked Shakespeare's Scottish Play as nothing else they had seen on this trip so far. It gave everyone chills, literally. Johnathon's wristwatch registered an air temperature of forty-five degrees, not counting the windchill. Despite the cold, the SOS were slow to get back on the bus. The wild beauty of the moor enthralled them.

At the end of the day, we arrived at the Palace Hotel in Inverness, our home for the next two nights. It was very nice, but after the time we had enjoyed at the Dunblane Hotel, we were all a little spoiled. Dinner proved to be another lesson that had not been covered back in Fairfax during the Cultural Sundays.

"I can't find anything to eat," said Libby, staring at the hotel's dinner menu.

"What's the problem?"

"It says that the lamb chops are served with something called neeps and tatties."

"That sounds like the names of a couple of kitty-cats," Nick remarked with a wink.

"Very funny, but I'm not eating something called a neep."

Deep sigh. "Okay, people, this menu is traditional Highland fare. Tatties are mashed potatoes. Neeps are simply mashed turnips."

"Well, why didn't they say so?" Libby persisted.

"Because we're in Scotland," Steve growled. He hadn't eaten anything for at least an hour, and he was starving.

"Yuck!" said Ellen. "I'm not eating turnips."

"Turnips are good," remarked Kurt, who seemed to be omnivorous. "I like them with butter. But what is this haggis?"

This is it. The dreaded question. "It's kind of a sausage." Did not have a clue what it really tasted like.

"What's in it?" Julie wanted to know.

Another sigh. "It's made of ground up meats like . . . um . . . sheep's liver."

A chorus of "euwes" greeted that bit of information.

"It's mixed with oatmeal, and lots of spices, and cooked in a casing like a sausage."

I omitted the fact that haggis was made up not only of liver, but also sheep's gizzards and lungs and that the casing was often the cleaned-out stomach lining of said sheep. I didn't want the SOS disgracing themselves in the middle of the Palace hotel's dining room. "Forget the haggis. Just ask for mince and tatties, and you'll be fine."

"What's mince? I thought that was a pie," Libby wanted to know.

"Mincemeat is a pie that we usually eat around Christmas and it's a dessert. Mince is another term for hamburger. If you ask for mince, you'll get hamburger."

There were twenty-three orders of mince and tatties with catsup. Kurt decided to be adventurous and actually try haggis. He manfully ate most of it, well-mixed within his mashed potatoes, turnips and a lot of catsup. Meanwhile, Ellen entertained everyone in the room with her balancing-a-spoon-on-the-end-of-your-nose trick. As the second youngest member of the team, Ellen looked like a fairy sprite, with her long blond hair and blue eyes. She had played the part of Puck in A MIDSUMMER NIGHT'S DREAM, and she was forgivably adorable while balancing a spoon on the end of her nose. Fortunately, after dinner, everyone was exhausted from a combination of castle crawling, fresh air on the moor and the Highlands' altitude. For once, we all went to bed early for a good night's sleep.

Or so I had hoped.

At two a.m. on July fifteenth, the telephone rang in our hotel room – a call from the United States. Instantly, Marty and I worried that our daughter at home had suffered some terrible accident.

"Hello, Mary? This is Mrs. Fox."

"Is it an emergency?" The Fox family lived next door to us. Was our house on fire?

"Oh, no, I just wanted to know if Jamie is all right. He hasn't phoned us since he left."

Grumble, grumble. Jamie never had time to phone home. We had been running around like headless chickens for a solid week. "He's fine. He's having a great time."

"I tried calling his room, but there was no answer." In other words, where is Jamie and what is he doing at this hour of the night?

"Jamie is asleep. He sleeps like the dead. We have trouble waking him up in the mornings."

"Oh, I thought he'd still be awake. It's a little early for him to go to sleep."

"Mrs. Fox, it's two in the morning here. Scotland is five hours ahead of you in Virginia."

"Oh! I didn't remember that. Sorry to wake you."

"I'll tell him you called in the morning. Good night, Mrs. Fox."

If Jamie is awake at seven in the morning, and he calls home at eight o'clock, he'll get his family up at three a. m. Eastern Daylight Time. Turnabout is fair play.

It took a long time for my heart rate to slow down so I could go back to sleep again.

By eight o'clock the next morning, all the kids were up, wolfing down huge breakfasts and were very, very excited. This was the day of the trip that everyone had talked about – other than the day of our cricket match, which now seemed like ancient history. Today we would be visiting Macbeth's Cawdor Castle, home of the Twenty-fifth and current Thane and Countess of Cawdor. Then we would make a stop at the Loch Ness Museum, and then the Loch itself, home of the legendary monster. Susan, who had dreamed of meeting the monster for the past five months, could barely sit still. The weather was once again grey and cool, but at least it wasn't raining – yet.

The drive to Cawdor was short, and along the way, we spotted some of Scotland's iconic shaggy Highland cattle. I am not partial to cattle as a general rule, but this breed with its long horns, long hair and adorable bangs over large, brown eyes could be classified as "cute."

More than any other place in Great Britain, Cawdor Castle is most associated with MACBETH. Glamis Castle was too civilized and not tucked away amid wild scenery like Cawdor was. Shakespeare, who never visited Scotland during his lifetime, described Cawdor Castle in these poetic words:

"This castle hath a pleasant seat, the air

Nimbly and sweetly recommends itself

Unto our gentle senses. . . .

The air is delicate."

One of the postcards in the Gift Shop, commissioned by the current Thane, who has a wry sense of humor, noted that "Cawdor Castle was begun in the fourteenth century which may be the reason why King Duncan was not murdered there in 1040."

The kids shivered with delicious horror as they investigated the moat, the spooky dungeon, and the "murder holes" above the main entrance, where boiling oil rained down on unwanted guests in the Middle Ages. The kids enjoyed climbing up the narrow, winding stone stairways to the towers and hanging over the castle's battlements. The gift shop was well-stocked with the best souvenirs seen to date. Some of the boys surreptitiously bought reproduction dirks, although none of them would admit to owning a weapon. Since we were touring in 1988, it was several years before the change of airplane regulations concerning sharp blades on board.

Next, we walked through the beautiful gardens that were in full summer bloom of riotous colors. Most of the kids had never seen, nor heard of, a foxglove plant. They squealed with shivers and delight to learn that foxgloves made not only a good heart medicine, but they were also deadly poisonous.

After the gardens, we had lunch, again in the castle café. While we were finishing up a delicious bread pudding dessert, Amy came back from the restroom, bursting with exciting news.

"Guess what?" she asked the chaperons.

It could be anything. I hoped it wasn't something furry – or dead. "What is it, Amy?"

She leaned closer, and said in a loud stage whisper, "The toilet paper in the bathroom! It's purple!" She giggled.

This piece of information created a rush to the restrooms. Upon investigation, we concurred that the castle's TP was indeed a deep lavender color. Everyone took some for their scrapbooks.

Before returning to the bus, we strolled over to a nearby field to see the Highland cattle at closer range. Susan sat on the fence, and tried to coax a grazing longhorn into coming over to her for a petting. The cow wasn't the least bit interested in a close encounter.

Like foxgloves and purple toilet paper, Highland cattle were something these kids had never seen before now. For Team SOS, sightseeing in Great Britain was definitely a lot more interesting than just castles and cathedrals.

From Cawdor, our next stop was the Loch Ness Monster Exhibition at Drumnadrochit, a small hamlet on the road beside the famous lake. The sun was beginning to burn through the clouds. We hadn't seen real sunshine since the day after our cricket game. The Official Loch Ness Monster Exhibition turned out to be your basic tourist trap, though it held some interest for the boys. Since this whole experience was totally tacky, I purchased a totally tacky plastic Loch Ness Monster toy. Most of the older girls by-passed the Exhibit altogether to visit the Scottish kilt shop next door. Brenda followed them to make sure they didn't take the place apart.

"Where did they get all their spending money?" she whispered as she slipped past me. "I thought they'd be dead broke by now."

"I think a lot of doting relatives sent checks. It sure wasn't what they earned washing cars."

Just down the road, Urquhart Castle was a romantic ruin standing on a knoll above Loch Ness. Its waters were supposed to be a favorite haunt of the monster. After visiting seven castles stuffed full of heavy furniture, epic paintings in gilded frames, walls hung with stag horns and naked swords and everything behind velvet-clad ropes, Urquhart Castle was a joyful relief. Its nooks and crannies provided a lot of fun for the kids to crawl over, under and around. It was a place to let them stretch their imaginations. The sun finally burst through the clouds with eye-searing brightness. From nowhere, it seemed, a bagpiper appeared in full kilts, and he stood on the hillside, playing a haunting tune. It was picture-perfect, and the beauty was not lost on Keene.

"Is this the day that all the castles send out their photographers for their postcards?" he quipped.

The bagpipe's music echoed off the surrounding hillsides and glens as we wandered around the ruins and down to the loch. I took my tacky, plastic Nessie to the pebbly shoreline of the lake, and anchored it in the water so that its head and tail stuck out. Then I laid down flat on the pebbles and took its picture, looking like the real Loch Ness Monster – as indeed it was now, since it was now "baptized" in the waters of the real Loch. Keene and Kathy, who had been watching with interest, asked if they could take Nessie's picture as well.

"You have to lie down flat, Kath," Keene advised.

"I am lying down flat."

"No, you're not. You're balancing on your elbows."

At this point more of the SOS teammates came down to the lake's shore.

"Hey," Julie called up to the rest of our mob. "We've got the monster down here."

General screaming and scrambling down the embankment. Once everyone caught on to the joke, they got out their cameras. The ensuing commotion attracted three Japanese tourists, who were just down the shingle beach, taking pictures of the opposite shoreline. They approached slowly, trying to see what was going on. After the last of the kids finished their monster photo op and went back up the hill to romp amid Urquhart's ruins, the Japanese smiled and pointed to the plastic Nessie and then to their cameras.

Nodding, "Yes, please do."

More huge smiles from the Japanese. They must have taken several dozen pictures from all angles except actually standing in the lake's freezing waters. Then, with much bowing and smiling they left. The day was perfect, the sky was bluer than any we had seen in Britain since we had landed, and the lake's waters, at least on the shoreline, were crystal clear. Thankfully, the real monster didn't put in an appearance.

After visiting eight stony castles in both England and Scotland, this ruin was the one that all the SOS said they liked the best. Perhaps it was because the ruins allowed the kids to wander in history with Shakespeare's plays as their guide. As the long afternoon waned, we gathered everyone back on the bus, did a nose count and left the real Loch Ness monster to swim in peace. Tacky, plastic Nessie was on his way to a new home in Virginia.

From Urquhart, it was back to Inverness for still more shopping. The following day, July Sixteenth, was Kurt's sixteenth birthday, so Marty and I located a bakery and got him a birthday cake, candles and a card.

The next day proved to be an unforgettable experience for Kurt.

Kurt never suspected that his teammates were about to spring an enormous surprise on him. Naturally, the ringleader and mistress of ceremonies was Kathy, but everyone joined in – except Kurt and the unsuspecting chaperones. Kathy, Susan and Terri spent the late afternoon in Inverness at a shop that sold colorful crepe paper streamers, balloons and party masks. After eating another "patties and mince" dinner at the Palace Hotel, the three girls, together with Keene, slipped away from their rooms and met with Chris at the carpark, as pre-arranged. For the next half hour, Keene blew up balloons while the girls draped the inside of the bus completely with the blue, orange, red and yellow party streamers.

The sixteenth of July was going to be the tour's Longest Day since we were driving back to London, a fourteen-hour non-stop journey south. Beginning around five in the morning, Keene, Steven and Jamie awakened Kurt with an early morning birthday celebration. Exactly what they ate or drank has never been revealed, although the words "beer shandies" slipped out, long after the fact. In any event, Kurt was delighted that someone had remembered his birthday.

After breakfast, Paul, Nick and all the girls disappeared quickly from the dining room, while Steve, Keene and Jamie distracted Kurt. Then, Kathy asked Marty and me to keep Kurt from getting on the bus until after everyone else was on board. First, we gave him the gift that his mom had slipped to me before we left Virginia. It was a woolen flat cap. Kurt was clueless when I told him that we needed to check all the rooms to make sure no one had forgotten anything. Kurt, always helpful, was glad to open doors to the empty rooms.

When we finally escorted the birthday boy onto the bus, everyone, including Brenda, Johnathon and Paul's mother, Marlene, were wearing bright-colored party masks, and singing "Happy Birthday" as loud as they could. Kurt was stunned and so very pleased to see all the decorations in his honor. But the fun didn't stop there. All eighteen girls had slathered on bright red lipstick and each one kissed Kurt, the team's romantic, very hard. His face, ears and neck were covered in red lip-prints. There was lots of applause and some presents. True SOS teamwork in action!

As Chris drove the bus out of the Highlands and into the Scottish Lowlands, Kurt slouched down in his seat, leaned against his window and fell asleep. After all, he had been up since five. His birthday cap was on his head, his face was still covered in lipstick and the little "Scottish Tribble," a furry critter from Ellen and Carol, sat on his shoulder.

It rained almost the entire way back to London – approximately 642 miles. At least, we were all warm, dry and not missing a lovely English summer day by being stuck on the bus. The coach had two major advantages: a bathroom and a video player with a large screen in the front. To while away the long hours on the road, the team saw "Heartbreak Hill," "The Sting" as well as episodes from the British sit-com, "Fawlty Towers" and "BBC Bloopers," which had everyone in fits of laughter.

Chris stopped at motorway rest stops every four hours where the kids loaded up on candy bars and other treats. During our lunch break, Kurt finally got to clean his face. For dessert, we surprised him with his birthday cake. Since the cake was frosted with Royal Icing that had hardened to a cement-like surface, the team was unable to smear frosting on his nose – a tradition that all the Shakespeareans observed at birthday celebrations and, years in the future, at some wedding receptions. Kurt tried to balance a sliver of the icing on the end of his nose, but gave it up after a few photos. He cut the cake with a knife that Marty had "liberated" from the breakfast table at the Palace Hotel. Kurt announced that he would get it engraved in honor of this momentous occasion. Knowing Kurt, he probably did. Zen finished carving the cake and she did a good job to get thirty pieces out of it. Meanwhile, several of the girls took down the balloons and disposed of the crepe paper, without being told. More SOS teamwork in action.

Then everybody settled down for naps and more movies as we rolled through the northern part of England. It remained quiet and peaceful on the bus, and, after a dinner stop on the motorway, we finally returned to our original hotel, the Ibis, at ten p.m.

It had been too quiet and too peaceful.

Shortly after midnight, Johnathon knocked on our door.

"Sorry to bother you, but I have to take Kathy to the hospital."

"What?" Wide awake. Heart pumping wildly. "What happened?"

"She hit her hand against a wall and hurt it pretty badly."

"How did she manage to do that?" Searched for the medical release forms that all the parents had filled out for their children to cover situations like this one.

"She was having a pillow fight with Keene and Steve."

Handing Kathy's medical permission slip to Johnathon. "A pillow fight? At this hour?"

"Yeah. They slept too much on the bus. I'll take care of her. You go back to sleep." Then he left.

Lying in the dark and staring up at the blank ceiling, I wondered how I was going to explain this caper to Kathy's mother. The minutes crawled by.

Two and a half hours later, Johnathon returned with Kathy, both of them extolling the virtues of Britain's National Health Service. A St. John's ambulance had taken them to the local emergency room, where Kathy was seen by a nurse, and an orderly, then the doctor and finally by the X-ray technician. She had been examined, x-rayed, taped up in a soft cast for her fractured wrist and given a small bottle of codeine pills for the pain. All Johnathon had to pay for was the taxi ride back to the hotel.

July seventeenth dawned rainy - again. With few exceptions, every day on this trip had been wet, but the weather hadn't dampened anyone's spirit. It was again Sunday, and a week since our famous cricket game. Brenda, Marlene and Johnathon took fourteen of the SOS to St. Paul's Cathedral for Sunday service and then on to the open-air street market of Petticoat Lane. Four of the group including Kathy wanted to sleep in, so only Elizabeth was game to go to Sunday Mass with Marty and me in a lovely Victorian Gothic church within walking distance of the hotel.

Later, upon their return, the other kids described St. Paul's as "great," the sermon was "weird," and they said that Petticoat Lane was "cheap and tacky." By this time, Day Twelve, I was really glad that our Epic Tour of Great Britain was just about over. Team SOS had a great time, had seen and done wonderful things and had played the game for which they had spent four months in practicing. But now I was tired of everything. Tired of planning and shepherding twenty-nine people. Tired of living out of a suitcase, and after only four hours of sleep the previous night, I was just plain tired. All I could do now was pray that we could get through the next thirty-six hours without any further incident.

CHAPTER TEN
July 18 - 31, 1988

"O brave, new world to have such people in it!"

The Tempest

The next morning dawned bright, sunny and warm – for once. The SOS spent their last day in England doing their two most favorite pastimes: eating and shopping. It was surprising that the kids still had any money left to spend after the glut of spending they had done in Scotland. This morning, all twenty-nine of us, chaperones included, hit Harrod's Department Store.

Harrod's is reputed to be the world's largest emporium; its seven-story building covers over five acres in Knightsbridge. It was once said that you could buy anything in the world at Harrod's. Shopping there was truly a destination experience. Twice a year, in January and July, Harrod's held major sales with deep discounts on its luxury goods. By pure dumb luck, the SOS happened to be in London during the summer Sales time.

Since it was possible to get completely lost inside this store, and cell phones had not yet become available, keeping the kids together was imperative. The chaperones divided up the team so that each of the adults could keep track of smaller groups, although I wound up with a party of eight: Paul, Susan, Amy, Molly, Terri, Kathy, and her two bodyguards, Keene and Steven. I told the boys that they had to carry everything for Kathy since she wasn't supposed to lift anything with her right hand. The two felt so guilty over Kathy's accident , they were her willing servants. We spent over three hours in Harrod's, mostly staring at the wealth of goods. The most popular items the team bought were things that had the Harrod's name and logo on them, like tea towels, key chains and coin purses.

Afterwards, we had lunch in Harrod's Upper Circle Restaurant, which still had reasonable prices at that time. From there, my group opted for yet more shopping at Covent Garden Market. Then, we met up with everyone else at the Cadogan Hotel for our formal English teatime experience.

The Cadogan on Sloane Street was where King Edward VII had secretly met with his mistress, Lillie Langtry. In fact, the hotel's restaurant was called Langtry's, and its walls were tastefully decorated with pictures of the Jersey Lily -- some of them were even autographed by her. Also pictured, near the bar, was author and wit Oscar Wilde, who had been arrested at the Cadogan and charged with sodomy in 1895. I did not share that bit of history with the kids. As advertised, the hotel and restaurant were beautifully appointed – lots of plants, mirrors and double-thickness tablecloths. The biggest disappointment was that instead of getting a full proper English Tea with finger sandwiches, scones, and sweets, we were just served a cup of tea with a slice of cake each.

The Cadogan was our travel agent's choice over my suggestion of the Café Royale. Derek had told me how really nice the Langtry restaurant was. My group had been looking forward to an English Tea experience, even if it had meant spending more. At this point, I let the problem slide by. After all, we had enjoyed a delicious English "bean feast" after the cricket game at Deddington. By now, all I could think about was getting everyone through the next twenty-four hours. We had an early evening, for once, and the team spent the time repacking their bulging suitcases.

Suddenly, it was July nineteenth, and our epic trip to Great Britain was almost at an end. By 10:15 a.m., Team SOS were in their seats on the bus, ready to go to the airport. Their heavy luggage had been crammed into the baggage compartment underneath us. Counting noses. Twenty-three kids?

"Listen up, people! Where's Meaghan? Has anybody seen her?"

Heads shake. "She wasn't at breakfast," Angelia volunteered.

"Okay, Keene, would you and Kathy please go back inside and find your sister?"

Throughout the trip, Meaghan had always been a little pokey. That was because she liked to absorb all the sights, sounds, colors, and experiences that were going on around her. But up until now, she had never missed roll call.

Keene returned in a few minutes, shaking his head. "She was still asleep. Kathy is moving her along."

We waited another ten minutes until Meaghan, slightly disheveled, arrived. Chris pushed her bulky suitcase into the luggage bin, then he hopped back into the driver's seat.

"Are we ready to go, boss lady?"

"Not just yet. Have to do a final passport check. All right, folks, passports in the air please. This is the final time."

Twenty-three passports waved in the breeze.

"Nick! Where is your passport?"

"I thought I didn't need it now that the trip is over."

"Nick, this is the most important time to have your passport. How do you expect to get back into the USA, if you don't have it? Where is it?"

"In my suitcase."

"Nick, you won't see your luggage again until after we go through Customs at Dulles Airport. You need your passport now." Turning to Chris. "Do you mind . . .?"

Chris was already out of his seat and back on the sidewalk, unlocking the luggage bin.

"Nick, go out and help him."

It was a good thing we started this trip to the airport early. This was the second time on the trip that Nick had packed his passport in his suitcase. Throughout the past two weeks Nick has alternated between using his razor-sharp mind and drifting off into the clouds. I think part of the problem was that he was older than everyone else, except Paul. Nick had now put his high school days far behind him. He was ready for college and had been wearing his James Madison University sweatshirt almost daily.

While we waited for him to retrieve his passport, I made a sweep through the overhead racks to see if anything was hidden up there. It was an interesting collection: a number of peacock feathers from the birds at Warwick Castle, three pairs of damp, dirty white socks left over from the cricket game, a room key from the Palace Hotel in Inverness that Steve thought he had lost, and several color photo booklets from Windsor and Warwick Castles that no one wanted. Brenda kept those. The peacock feathers were also claimed; the socks were not.

Finally, Nick was back in his seat with his passport; Chris was back behind the wheel. The bus door slammed shut one last time and we were off to Heathrow International Airport.

Chris was genuinely sorry to say goodbye to the SOS His eyes even looked a little moist when he said how much fun he had with us; that we were the best tour he had ever driven. That was probably because he usually drove people over the age of fifty. We gave him two sports pennants from the Washington [DC] football team, and he seemed very happy to get them. We also tipped him one hundred and ten pounds and gave him a card that everyone had signed. He was the very best driver we could have had.

Once we got everyone through the Security Check and were seated in the Boarding Lounge, I began to relax. Then Terri whispered to me that she couldn't find her boarding pass. Marty managed to get another one for her, but that excitement left her shaken for quite a while.

Then Kurt whispered to us that he had found an odd, green-beaded necklace in his SOS duffle bag that had not been there at the Security checkpoint. It looked like Middle Eastern worry beads, very badly made and painted. The idea flashed through my mind that the beads could be made of some drug, like cocaine. I told Kurt to bury the beads in the trash bin and then sit close to us.

In retrospect, perhaps we should have given them to airport security, but at the time, I thought that would involve a lot of questions and running around, and Kurt, who had thought the same thing, was already a little unglued. We told him that we would stick close to him at Dulles until his parents picked him up.

A few of the girls were upset about going back home and they sat apart with tears in their eyes. One of them knew she was going to be packed off to a job at a summer day camp that her mom had arranged for her, to keep her busy and out of the house during the rest of the summer. She hated the whole idea. Another one was returning to a sticky home situation that had probably not been resolved while she had been away in England.

Sabrina accidently bumped her nose on something, and now had a nosebleed. Brenda got her some ice, and a couple of damp paper towels and told her to sit down and not move.

A lot of the kids made last-minute visits to the candy and news stand. Meaghan bought a few more of her beloved British magazines. She had already paid an overweight fine for the extra forty pounds of magazines that she had collected during the past two weeks.

One of the girls announced that she wanted to go through the Value Added Tax return line to get the refund of the sales taxes she had paid for all her shopping. She had saved all her receipts. None of the other kids had bothered to do that. Marty said he would take care of it and he went off to get the VAT form, but then Terri's lost boarding pass took precedence and Marty disappeared with her. Nothing more was said about the VAT tax refund money until just before we were about to board the plane. At that point, it was too late to do anything about it. At the very most, she would have gotten back three dollars and fifty cents. When she realized that she wasn't going to get any money back, she stalked ahead of everyone and stayed in a royal sulk all the way onto the plane. She had gone through several of these snit fits during the past two weeks, when she pulled away from everyone and looked mad or pouty. By this time, I had enough of adolescent moods. After we boarded, I slipped her four dollars to cover the VAT and told her to quit sulking. There was enough on my mind with Kathy's fractured wrist, two girls in tears, Sabrina's bloody nose that had finally stopped running and Kurt's mysterious beads.

Thank heavens, Kaija was our seat mate, together with her new white teddy bear that she had named Snug, after Snug, the Joiner from A MIDSUMMER NIGHT'S DREAM. Kaija had been wonderful during the entire trip – always bubbly and happy. She never seemed to be upset about anything, not even getting soaked and cold during the cricket game. Just before take-off, I looked around the cabin to make sure that all twenty-four kids were present and accounted for. I spied Becky wearing one of the party masks from Kurt's birthday surprise – and Nick's James Madison U. sweatshirt. Molly had on her red ballcap -- and a rubber mouse nose, purchased at Covent Garden.

Only seven more hours to go!

All of their parents were waiting behind the barrier at Dulles International Arrivals. Some waved posters that said "Welcome Home!" and others held balloons. Marty and I walked with Kurt between us, but no one took any interest in him or his duffle bag, except his parents. Molly wore her mouse nose through Passport Control and out to the Arrivals lounge. Her parents didn't seem the least surprised to see her latest fashion accessory. Kathy's mom was very understanding about Kathy's wrist and didn't threaten to sue, although she took charge of the bottle of codeine pills. Sabrina had forgotten all about her bloody nose. And the weepy girls were all smiles to see their folks and siblings.

Marty and I went home, hugged our daughter and our dog, ordered pizza for dinner, took hot baths and slept away the next fourteen hours.

Shortly after we returned to Virginia, Bill Drake, wrote a letter of thanks for bringing the SOS to Deddington:

The Most Improbable International Cricket Team Ever: A True Story

"To see your lot run out on that soggy, wind-blown meadow did my old bones good and I've been playing the game for a long time. They were young, keen, lively and fresh – a great bunch; a credit to you and to your country. I look forward to the next game. Wouldn't it be nice if we could do the thing in reverse and get a bit of poison ivy in OUR veins? A pipe dream, but who knows? Maybe one of these days we might have enough money to do it!"

It was all over but the shouting, which, knowing the Shakespeareans Over Seas, was going to go on for a long time to come. After washing five loads of laundry, including our mud-stiffened pants from the cricket game, sleeping heavily for the next several days, and waiting for the jet lag to wear off, it was time for the Wrap-Up parties. All in all, it had been a great trip. Team SOS had been noisy, creative in their jokes and schemes, mega shoppers, culturally inclined [which was a pleasant surprise], had fewer personality "flare-ups" than expected, were more "other-directed" than "inner directed," used lots of band-aids, some Tylenol, and everyone could boast of a few little side-adventures that had been off the grid.

A week after we returned to Fairfax County, Marty and I hosted a picture-exchange party called the Grab. Everyone showed up, photo packets in hand, even Kathy, who had gotten her wisdom teeth extracted that morning. The party was an overwhelming success and the noise level was incredible. I had asked everyone to get double prints of their photos: one set to keep and one set to bring to the Grab. All the photos were put in a wide pile in the middle of our family room floor, and when everyone was ready, they were given the word to dive in and take what they wanted. There were literally hundreds of photos spread out all over the rug.

"Who took this?"

"Can I trade you this pic of Hever Castle for that one of Cawdor?"

"Oh, I look a wreck! Did I really run around the Tower of London with half my shirt hanging out?"

"How did you get this picture of me sleeping on the bus! Who took this? Do I really sleep with my mouth open?"

"Oh, look at this one of the peacocks at Warwick! You mean I can keep this one? Ohh, thanks!"

"Look at us at the game! Look at the trees bending almost double! Was it really that windy?"

"Does anyone have a picture of me when I'm actually smiling?"

"Why did you have to take one of me eating?"

"Paul! You take the best pictures! Wow!"

"Look how muddy we all got at the cricket game."

"Are we having any snacks soon, Mrs. Schaller?"

"Yes."

On the following Saturday evening, Steve's family hosted the trip's Show 'n' Tell party, not only for the SOS, but especially for their parents. In order to encourage the kids to get immersed in the trip, they had been asked to create projects for Show-And-Tell at this party. The parents wanted to see and experience their children's adventures, and the projects were the best way to do it. All but Julie came. She was in Texas, visiting with her father, but her mother attended the Wrap-Up on Julie's behalf.

Some of the kids had already put together scrapbooks, using the pictures they had taken at the Grab. The best book was the one that Keene and Steve had created. They had obviously grabbed all the good pictures and their work was neatly captioned. Kurt displayed his cricket library that he had quietly gathered along the way. He also showed his extensive bookmark collection and a beautiful model of the Tower of London, complete with tiny ravens on the lawn. Elizabeth had bought reproductions of the Crown Jewels from the Tower gift shop, and she proudly displayed them on a red velvet background.

Jamie made a poster collage of all the various candy wrappers he had gathered on the trip. It was colorful, artistic and mind-boggling, when you consider the amount of sugar and chocolate he must have consumed. Meaghan brought a sampling of the British magazines from her collection. She arranged her stash with the most interesting and colorful covers in front. A lot of the mothers scanned through those. Angela made a poster about St. Catherine's College, using postcards, a menu from dinner, and other various bits and pieces she had gleaned from the dorm's trash bin. Kym had collected interesting pebbles and candle wax drippings from every place we had been, and she made a display coupling the stones and wax with photos or postcards of the original locale.

Amy's toilet paper collection was the most unusual poster. Not only was the Cawdor purple TP on show, but so were several sheets from the Tower of London's loo. Each sheet had the words "Property of HM The Queen" stamped on them. Other samples exhibited the wide variety of textures and thicknesses of Great Britain's restroom paper offerings.

The kids danced a comic version of the Highland Fling that they had learned in Dunblane. Steve, Keene, Terri and Susan did a very funny skit titled "Waking Up The Boys." The Team gave flowers to all the chaperones. Keene, as the SOS Team captain, presented Johnathon with a real silver cricket trophy that the kids had found in a second-hand shop in Oxford. Johnathon was both surprised and pleased. Marty and I got matching cricket-themed mugs from Harrods. Steve's mom gave me a framed brass plaque with the SOS logo etched on it. All the girls cried when the party broke up. Everyone hugged everyone else. Kurt went around for second embraces from the girls.

Then Team SOS returned to their real lives. Kathy's wrist healed in time for her to attend field hockey camp. Little Susan finally got her braces off. Jamie went out of town to visit relatives. Nick started madly packing and buying dorm supplies since he was due to start his college career in three short weeks.

And no one could believe how fast July 1988 had flown by.

Teammates Elizabeth Dettmar and Kaija Barlow get out of the rain by the Deddington pavilion. The board does not record the actual final score of the game. Witney got 61 runs; the SOS got 11. (Mary Schaller)

EPILOGUE
All's *Well That Ends Well*

"Give me your hands if we be friends."
A Midsummer Night's Dream

"The purpose of making the trip isn't just to take in the sights," I had told the JOURNAL reporter in June 1988. "We wanted to get to know the people over there and we thought [cricket] would be a great way to do it." The team's goal had been met far better than anyone had expected. Many of the kids had exchanged addresses with the Witney Swim Club members. Kym, for one, kept up with her pen-friend for over eight years.

"Stuart Knight – we were in touch until 1994 or so. I visited him when I lived in London in 1992. He was at the Glasgow School of Art, and I spent a week hanging out with him and his friends."

Terri maintained a long-term pen-friendship with Mack McCormack. She visited him in the 1990s and then returned to England several years later to celebrate his wedding. As of 2019, Terri and Mack were still sending Christmas cards to each other. "I most recently saw him two or three years ago," Terri wrote in February 2021.

Other team members kept up with their new Witney friends for at least a year after that epic game in the mud. Carol didn't write to any of the Witneys. She was younger than they were, but she did exchange addresses with the boy she had danced with all through the night in Dunblane.

"Michael was Scottish, " she recalled. "He was staying at the hotel with his Granny. Michael and I were pen pals for quite a while after that, but [we] lost track of each other over the years."

Mary W. Schaller

The trip also expanded everyone's life experiences. Susan, the Mighty Mite, echoed the general feelings of the Team: "I will never forget this trip. I have grown as a person from it, and I met very special people. I had the time of my life!"

The usual British tour route of the Tower of London, Harrod's, St. Paul's Cathedral, Oxford colleges, Glamis & Urquhart castles, Petticoat Lane, Stratford and Hadrian's Wall were merely backdrops to the SOS unique experiences. It was the unexpected moments that lingered with them long after they returned home. Things like wild purple thistles, cow patties, poisonous foxgloves, purple TP at Cawdor Castle, a plastic Nessie in Loch Ness, Whispa Bars & Smarties chocolates, telling ghost stories all night long in Stratford, talking on the BBC radio, punting on the river in Oxford, dumpster diving at St. Catz, Scottish dancing at Dunblane Hotel, playing frisbee at Hadrian's Wall, neeps & tatties, stalking peacocks at Warwick, Kurt's birthday party, channeling MACBETH on the moor at Culloden and most of all, playing the rain-soaked cricket game with the Whitney swim team.

Above everything else, the trip cemented life-long friendships that the SOS team had made with each other – friendships that had begun on a muddy field with a ball, a bat and a wicket.

*   *   *   *

Over thirty years later, Team SOS is still the Undefeated Co-ed Cricket Champion of Fairfax County, Virginia.

FOREVER YOUNG!

Top step: Kym Samuels

Next step down: [L to R] Angela Kluwin and Elizabeth Dettmar

Third step down: [L to R] Nick Rose and Ellen Caskie

Fourth step down: [L to R] Paul Miller, Jamie Fox and Kurt Bose

Fifth Step down: [L to R] Zen Mason, Molly Pfaff, Kaija Barlow, Sabrina Sandusky and Meaghan Parker.

Sixth step down: Susan Linsert

Seventh Step down: [L to R] Becky Kelsey, Kathy Robinson, Keene Parker and Amy Pearson

Bottom step: [L to R] Libby Goodwin, Katie Shirley, Steven Fender, Terri Anderson and Julie Zielaskiewicz. Absent: Carol Blosser. (Anderson Family collection)

APPENDEX

THE S.O.S. CRICKET TEAM MEMBERS

July 10, 1988

Deddington Cricket Club, Deddington, Oxfordshire, England

The First Eleven – plus two

As they appeared in batting order:

Jamie Fox – Bowler

Keene Parker, Team Captain – Bowler

Kathy Robinson – 1st Slip

Kurt Bose – Bowler

Terri Anderson – Wicket-keeper

Steve Fender – Cover Point

Kaija Barlow – Wicket Keeper & 2nd Slip

Molly Pfaff – Gully

Zen Mason – Mid-off

Susan Linsert – Bowler

Amy Pearson – Long Leg

Extra "Men"

Katie Shirley – Long Leg

Elizabeth Dettmar – Mid-on

Coach – Johnathon Bigelow Manager – Mary Schaller

Scorekeeper – Kym Samuels

The Most Improbable International Cricket Team Ever: A True Story

The Second Eleven – minus one

Julie Zielaskiewicz – Team Co-Captain & Scorekeeper

Carol Blosser – Square Leg

Ellen Caskie – Deep Point

Libby Goodwin – Third Slip

Becky Kelsey -- Cover

Angela Kluwin – Fine Leg

Paul Miller – Team Photographer

Meaghan Parker -- Sweeper

Nick Rose – Assistant Manager

Sabrina Sandusky – Cow Corner

"We are such stuff as dreams are made on, and our little life is rounded with a sleep."

Shakespeare's THE TEMPEST

Kaija Barlow with Jamie Fox asleep on her shoulder on the bus after the game at Deddington Cricket Field. (Paul Miller)

BIBLIOGRAPHY

Books

_____. *Cricket. Tips from Sporting Heroes.* Oxford, England: PAST TIMES. 2003.

_____. *Laws of Cricket.* London: Marylebone Cricket Club. 1980.

Diagram Group. *Rules of the Game.* London: Diagram Visuals, Information Ltd., Paddington Press Ltd., 1974.

Eastway, Robert. *Cricket Explained.* New York: St. Martin's Press, 1992.

Formhals, Hugh. *The Jolliest Game Under The Sun: A Beginner's Guide To Cricket.* WesternMountain Press. 1984.

Grosvernor, Melvin Bell & Franc Shor, editors. *This England.* National Geographic Society.

Chicago: National Geographic Society, R. R. Donnelley and Sons Co. 1966.

Southgate, V., M.A., B. Comm. *The Story of Cricket. A Ladybird 'Easy Reading' Book.*

Loughborough, England: Willis & Hepworth, Ltd. 1964.

Articles and Newspapers

Bell, Robert. "Cricket Finds N. Va." *The Fairfax Journal,* June 20, 1988.

Mary W. Schaller

Drake, Bill. "U.S. Cricketers." *The Banbury GUARDIAN.* July 4, 1988.

Drake, Bill. "Cricket at Deddington." *The Banbury GUARDIAN.* July 14, 1988.

Graves, Gary. "Cricket Anyone?" *The Washington [DC] times.* June 15, 1988.

ACKNOWLEDGEMENTS

This short book was born during the coronavirus pandemic of 2020. While going through old photographs, I happened upon my scrapbook from the summer of 1988, when I was the manager of a co-ed, teenage, American cricket team. That adventure had been one of those unexpected and unforgettable experiences. Writing the book took me away from the four walls of my quarantine apartment, and back to Rutherford Park in Fairfax County, Virginia with the summer's hot, humid afternoons, poison ivy on all sides, and a muddy creek that liked to suck up cricket balls. Turning the pages of that scrapbook, I could hear in my memory each team member's voice . . . their laughter, their banter and most of all, their yelling. They were a loud, exuberant bunch. After the passage of so many years, I felt that their story was one that should not be left to molder away inside an old box. The young members of the SOS were like a combination of the Little Engine That Could and the Bad News Bears Baseball Team. The kids grabbed onto a wild, improbable idea and, through their sheer will power – and, with a lot of help from a British diplomat, a Pakistani cricket buff, an English cricket fan and a charming Kiwi from New Zealand, they did it.

Just as it takes a team to play cricket, it took a team to help me write this book. I am deeply grateful to the former SOS team members who kindly sent me their memories: Kym Samuels Crow, Terri Anderson Hitchingham, Paul Miller and Carol Blosser Fanning, as well as Lisa Moore, Brenda Bigelow, and team coach, Johnathon Bigelow. Special thanks go to my critique circle: Virginia and Harry Day, and Marcy and Don Leverenz. Their encouragement, suggestions and, most especially, their enthusiasm for this book were especially helpful.

Four decades later, I send my much-belated gratitude to all the parents of Team SOS. Without their help and tremendous support, the SOS would have never made it to England, nor ever played cricket. More belated gratitude goes to the Deddington Cricket Club for hosting the SOS – Witney game in July 1988, and especially to Mr. and Mrs. Dobson who supplied the delicious tea and who umpired in a gale. Most special thanks and appreciation are due to the late Bill Drake, President of the Deddington Cricket Club, without whom this midsummer night's dream would never have taken place. Finally, none of this adventure would have been possible without the help and support of my wonderful, patient husband, Marty Schaller. He walked every step of the way with me in 1988, and he continues to do so to the present day. His memories of the trip and the epic game were especially helpful, his editing of this manuscript and the cropping of the photos was a godsend.

Springfield, Virginia
February 2021

ILLUSTRATIONS

The author is deeply grateful for the use of so many images from the photo albums of Johnathon Bigelow, Paul Miller, Terri Anderson-Hitchingham, The Linsert Family and Martin Schaller.

ABOUT THE AUTHOR

MARY W. SCHALLER is a native of Washington, DC [remaining staunchly non-partisan for survival.] She earned her Bachelor of Arts degree in Theatre Arts from the University of San Diego and, prior to her marriage, she worked in the Communications Department of Metro-Goldwyn-Mayer Studio in Culver City, Ca. For twenty years she was a docent at the Folger Shakespeare Library in Washington, DC. During that time, she also directed 21 play productions for Fairfax County [VA] Followspot Children's Theater, including 17 plays of Shakespeare. She is the award-winning author of five plays [Dramatic Publishing Co. and Heartland Plays, Inc.], three non-fiction books [University of South Carolina Press] and ten historical

Mary W. Schaller

romance novels, written as Tori Phillips [Harlequin Ltd.] Schaller's novels have been translated into fourteen languages and they have collectively sold nearly three million copies world-wide. Her plays have been performed not only in the United States, but also in Canada, Australia and England. Mary lives with Martin, her husband of fifty-five years, in Springfield, VA. Her hobbies include cruising the Caribbean, reading books and racing radio-controlled sailboats.